Let's keep it
the best

MW00696289

Pastor Jackie

BAD BOSSES

LESSONS FOR LEADERS

JACKIE ALLEN

Foreword by Chris Sonksen

BAD BOSSES
Published by Kopi Books
105B 5555 Youngstown Warren Road
Niles, OH 44446 U.S.A.

Unless otherwise noted, all Scripture quotations are taken from the Holman Christian Standard Bible® Copyright © 1999, 2000, 2002, 2003 by Holman Bible Publishers. Used by permission. Holman Christian Standard Bible®, Holman CSB®, and HCSB® are federally registered trademarks of Holman Bible Publishers.

Scripture quotations marked NIV are from the Holy Bible, New International Version®, NIV® Copyright © 1973, 1978, 1984, 2011 by Biblica, Inc.® Used by permission. All rights reserved worldwide.

Scripture quotations marked (NLT) are taken from the Holy Bible, New Living Translation, copyright ©1996, 2004, 2015 by Tyndale House Foundation. Used by permission of Tyndale House Publishers, Carol Stream, Illinois 60188. All rights reserved.

Scripture quotations marked KJV are from The King James Version. Public Domain.

ISBN 978-0-578-82137-5
Copyright © 2021 by Jackie Allen

Design: Lydia Tarleton

Printed in the United States of America 2021

This book is dedicated to my faithful wife who has believed in me and encouraged me since our days as high school sweethearts. To my kids who have taught me more than I could ever teach them. To my staff who has been the laboratory for the principles taught in this book. And to my coach who challenged me to put these principles into print.

WHAT PEOPLE ARE SAYING ABOUT *BAD BOSSES*...

"North America needs godly leaders. I can think of no better place to learn how to develop the leadership skills we need in this unique moment of history than God's Word. Jackie Allen's new book Bad Bosses provides great insights into the strengths and weaknesses of some of the most significant leaders in the Bible. I'm excited to see how God will use leaders in North America as they apply the principles, he describes to impact their communities."

Kevin Ezell
President
North American Mission Board, SBC

"This is a book that has been needed for a long time. The world and the church have suffered at the hands of numerous bad bosses over the years. It is time we learn what to look for in a boss, what to avoid as a boss, and how to be the kind of boss God wants us to be—more like Jesus! This is a great, biblical survey of the lessons we can learn to keep from following in the footsteps of the infamous Kings of Israel. I highly recommend it!"

Dr. David Johnson
Executive Director
Arizona Southern Baptist Convention

"In his book, Bad Bosses, my friend Jackie tackles the biggest problem all leaders eventually have to face - themselves. Throughout these pages, you will find principles that will set you free from leadership limitations and put you on a course to become the boss you were meant to be."

Chris Sonksen
Pastor of South Hills
Founder of Church Boom

"If you have any desire to grow as a leader you must read this book! It's practical, helpful, and worth every moment you give to it. Jackie knocked it out of the park on this one!"

Doug Garasic
Best Selling Author
Pastor of Rust City Church

"I have known Pastor Jackie for more than 25 years. He has been my pastor, my mentor, and my boss. His insights into Godly leadership have consistently born fruit in his own life and ministry. He is a champion of encouraging, investing in, and challenging young leaders to follow the leadership of Jesus. Anyone interested in learning how to lead like Jesus should grab this book and study it!"

Rayden Hollis
St. Louis Send City Missionary
North American Mission Board
Lead Pastor of Red Hill Church in Edwardsville, IL

"Jackie's direct investment in me as a young leader 25-years ago continues to guide my approach to leading today. This book will help guide yours."

Rusty Gunn
Founding Pastor
A Church That Matters

"Bad Bosses is not leadership theory, but hard-won wisdom from decades of organizational leadership in a ministry setting. You'll enjoy the honest raw style and gain much from biblical principles applied to leadership."

Brian Bowman
Founder Valley Life Network

"Jackie's insight into the life of a leader has roots deep in his own leadership journey. He has taken truths from the greatest leadership manual of all time and has equipped leaders of all types and pointed them to the greatest leader of people, Jesus Christ. I am thankful to have this book as a resource in my own personal leadership journey."

David Starry
Lead Pastor
First Light Church, Vandalia, Ohio

CONTENTS

FORE WORD

BY CHRIS SONKSEN

Early in my career, I experienced what some might define as a bad boss. I was one of the employees on staff at a church that appeared to be winning. Our boss had experienced decent success over the years, but I quickly realized that success was being limited. It wasn't resources that prohibited the church's advancement. In fact, they were doing well financially. They didn't lack clear strategy, and there was nothing wrong with their organizational structure.

They actually had many things going right for them; including resources, talented team members, and a strong reputation. On a surface level, they had all the right elements for exponential success. So why weren't they experiencing it? You've probably already guessed it! They had a bad boss.

From the outside, you wouldn't know anything was wrong. The leader had integrity, communicated well, could cast vision, and rally a crowd. But when you pulled back the curtain and took a closer look, you found bad boss traits that kept the team, and ultimately the ministry, from reaching their potential.

The worst of those traits was insecurity. The boss couldn't stand it when his team would start to shine. I saw firsthand how he would maneuver whatever necessary to extinguish their light and minimize their impact. It would often happen in staff meetings. Whenever an employee would appropriately push back or give another opinion, he would respond defensively, causing others to shut down. Sometimes other traits - pride and jealousy - would show their hand as well. It prohibited the team from functioning at their fullest capacity. These bad boss traits kept individuals from advancing, the team from growing, and ultimately limited the church from reaching its God-given potential.

My friend, Jackie Allen, tackles this subject in his latest book, Bad Bosses. Throughout these pages, you will find principles that will set you free from leadership limitations and put you on a course to become the boss you were meant to be. Too often, God-honoring ministries and businesses, who are overflowing with possibilities, hit their lid prematurely. It's not because there's a lack of opportunity, but rather because of opposition from a bad boss.

You may have heard it said, "If you want to go fast, go alone. If you want to go far, go with a team." I believe that every leader's heart has a desire to go far - taking their church or business to places it's never been. But often, we as leaders hold our own organizations back because of damaging behaviors that continue to run our lives. In essence, we become the lid to our very own team and organization. One of the greatest tasks of a leader is to define reality. And part of defining reality is taking a hard look at ourselves in the mirror and evaluating the type of boss we really are. The most helpful self-assessments are honest ones. They ask the question, "Would I want to work for me?"

I challenge you to let this book take you on a journey of self-evaluation. Let it serve as a light that shines into the secret places of your heart and reveals the traits that may be holding you back. I one-hundred-percent believe God has designed and purposed you for greatness. You were created to do mighty works. Don't settle by continuously operating with actions and behaviors that sabotage who you are and what you will become. Read through these pages, ask the tough questions, and take your team through this book. Approach these principles with an open and honest heart. If you do, God can help you overcome bad boss traits that are limiting your impact and influence. This book has been brilliantly written. It contains God-centered ideas and life-changing concepts - what you do with them is up to you. My advice: go all in.

WHERE DO BOSSES COME FROM?

Sometimes the best life lessons are learned from examples of what not to do instead of what to do. For example, when we see someone wasting their life with drugs or alcohol, we start to think about staying away from those substances. Suppose we witness a relationship implode because of poor choices. We might be motivated to make better choices in an attempt to make our relationships stronger.

Why learn from your mistakes when you can learn from the mistakes of others? Don't get me wrong - we can surely learn from our mistakes, but we don't have to solely learn from our mistakes. We can learn even more from the mistakes of others. That is the premise of this book. We are going to learn from the mistakes of others, particularly bosses and leaders. By looking at their mistakes, we can find practical ways to avoid the same pitfalls.

Throughout Bad Bosses, we'll dive into the lives of several kings in the Old Testament. When it came to Old Testament kings, we discover that they made many mistakes that we can learn from. Imagine you worked in an office for the past 10 years; each of those years, you had a new boss, and each new boss was worse than the one before. You started out with Michael Scott from The Office, and it all went downhill from there. It's hard to even imagine! But that is pretty much the story of the nation of Israel in the Old Testament. They wanted a king to rule them, but somehow each one was a worse leader than the one who led before him. Here's a great example:

But Omri did evil in the eyes of the LORD and sinned more than all those before him. (1 Kings 16:25, NIV)

And so, the story goes with all of the kings - aka bosses, of Israel. Surely, we can learn some things from these guys as we seek to become better bosses and leaders.

Let's start with the origins of Israel's monarchy and their desire for a king. It will help us understand why we are sometimes bad bosses or why we often look to bosses or leaders to do more than intended.

In 1 Samuel, the idea of a boss or king started. We're introduced to the first King of Israel, Saul. In chapter one, we find out that Saul was an insecure boss.

WE WANT A KING (BOSS) – BE CAREFUL WHAT YOU ASK FOR!

This whole story starts with Israel asking for a king:

So all the elders of Israel gathered together and went to Samuel at Ramah. They said to him, "Look, you are old, and your sons do not follow your example. Therefore, appoint a king to judge us the same as all the other nations have."

When they said, "Give us a king to judge us," Samuel considered their demand sinful, so he prayed to the Lord. But the Lord told him, "Listen to the people and everything they say to you. They have not rejected you; they have rejected Me as their king. They are doing the same thing to you that they have done to Me, since the day I brought them out of Egypt until this day, abandoning Me and worshiping other gods. (1 Samuel 8:4-8)

YOUR BOSS, YOUR KING, OR YOUR POLITICAL LEADER WILL NEVER BE YOUR SAVIOR.

Your boss, your king, or your political leader will never be your savior. Anytime we sinfully look to a leader to answer our problems, we are, in essence, rejecting God. Many times, our problems with our bosses and leaders are actually problems within us. We may expect far more from them than what they can provide. Although they may have been given authority by God, they can't fulfill God's role as the ultimate leader of your life.

Your primary boss, your primary king, and your primary Lord should be Jesus Christ. He is the boss of our lives. That's why Paul writes in Philippians 2:10-11 (NLT) that one day "every knee should bow...and every tongue confess that Jesus Christ is Lord." The Greek word for Lord literally means boss or supreme authority.

And so, the request for a king was sinful on the part of the people. Why? Because they wanted to replace God with an earthly leader.

I WILL GIVE YOU A KING (BOSS) - BE CAREFUL WHAT YOU SAY YES TO!

After their big ask, God made a reluctant concession and granted their wish for a king. It wasn't his plan A; it was plan B. The Bible spoke of this when Samuel relayed the people's desire for a king to God:

> *"Listen to them," the Lord told Samuel. "Appoint a king for them." (1 Samuel 8:22)*

God gave in after multiple requests, and the Israelites ended up anointing Saul as their first king. And let me tell you, this dude had some issues! I mean, he was messed up on all sorts of levels. He disobeyed God time and time again - always leading from a place of pride and insecurity instead of humility.

But before we go any further, I want to call a timeout to remind you that this book isn't intended to bash bosses. If you bought this book with hopes of circulating it at your office, attempting to change or get rid of your boss - you are going to be disappointed.

The truth is we are all bosses of something or someone. At the very least, we are called to lead ourselves. The hope is that we can learn from others' failures and successes to become better bosses - whether that's of others or ourselves.

At the very least, I hope you come to appreciate how hard it is to be the boss and lead. I've found from personal experience that it can often be a lonely position.

If you've never been the boss, but you're critical of your boss - please remember that leadership is difficult. It's impossible to know the full extent of that difficulty until you've walked in those shoes. So for those of you who haven't, let me try to help you through what I've learned. Here are four reasons why being the boss is extremely difficult:

#1 - All Bosses Lead Sinners

All bosses lead sinners. I mean, a sinner is the best description of everyone in your workplace, including yourself. Before you throw your boss under the bus, remember he leads people who are just like you and me. We are sinners. We have the capacity to mess up, and often!

The best description of spiritual leadership in the Bible that I can think of is the illustration of a shepherd and his sheep. People love that visual and are drawn to it. Murals have been painted to illustrate it, and postcards have been created to depict it. We stereotypically see a shepherd out in a lily field leading a group of fluffy, innocent sheep. It comes across as a beautiful, peaceful, and pleasant pastoral scene.

And yet, Jeff Iorg, in his book, *The Painful Side of Leadership*, says this: "The reality is sheep bite, they run amok, they get diseases, they wander into trouble, they're attacked by wolves. They do dumb things, even the seemingly smart ones. They injure themselves often blaming the shepherd and they nip at each other."[1]

I love the picture that paints of what shepherding is actually like. What Jeff describes is the workplace environment that your boss is challenged to lead. They're in charge of many stinky sheep who run amok, get diseases, wander into trouble, and do dumb things.

Every boss is in charge of a bunch of sinners. So, before you boss bash, just remember that they have the tough job of leading people like you and me!

#2 - All Bosses Are Sinners

To make matters worse, not only do all bosses lead sinners, all bosses are sinners. This is true of bosses in both the secular and sacred world. Your pastor, or boss, struggles with the same temptations you do. Our own sin contributes to the pain we experience as leaders. But it goes even further than that. Their sin not only negatively affects them but potentially negatively affects those they lead, as well. This, in large part, is what leaders know as living in the proverbial fishbowl. The fishbowl effect is the reality that everything a leader does is observable and examined by those around them. Because of this, leaders carry the burden of knowing our sinful choices can create painful consequences for ourselves and those we lead. And that can be pretty daunting!

#3 - All Bosses Lead in a Fallen World

On top of the fact that all bosses lead sinners and are sinners, they also lead in a fallen world.

Sometimes - actually many times - the problems that exist in your workplace are not the fault of your boss or fellow employees. Problems are inevitable - they'll always exist! It's not always the bosses' or employee's fault; it just is.

Think about this hypothetical example: A tsunami can hit the coast of Asia, delaying the work of shipping companies. Suddenly, halfway across the globe at your workplace, you have a distribution problem. Was it your boss' fault? No. Was it the employee's fault? No. Was it the shipping company's fault, even? Absolutely not. We just live in a fallen world where we have tsunamis, hurricanes, earthquakes, fires, and floods. Sometimes your boss is dealing with issues beyond his or her control, simply because we live in a fallen world.

This is equally true of leadership in the church world. I'm currently writing this book in 2020. This year, we've experienced a global pandemic that's nearly shut down the world's economy. If this year has taught us anything, it's that we live and lead in a fallen world. For example, suppose your pastor closed your church building for months and required you to wear a mask when you returned in response to the pandemic. Even if you disagree with it being handled that way, you must admit those are tough calls that leaders are forced to make! They didn't ask to have to decide on those types of matters. It's a product of leading in a clearly flawed and fallen world.

#4 - All Bosses are Under Attack

This is especially true of Christian bosses and Christian leaders, but I think it's true of all bosses. If the enemy can derail you as the leader, he can derail many others. If he can negatively affect the leader, there will be a domino effect of negativity throughout the entire organization.

Your battle Monday through Friday at work is not with flesh and blood. We may think that the two-legged devil we call our boss is the source of our problems. That's because we've bought into the myth that our battle is with flesh and blood. But the Bible teaches us otherwise. It says, "our struggle is not against flesh and blood...but against spiritual forces of evil in the heavenly realms." (Ephesians 6:12, NIV) So instead of complaining about your boss, your leader, or your pastor, it might be more effective to pray for them.

As we prepare to dive into case studies throughout the Old Testament on some bad bosses, I want to challenge you to not put too much faith and trust in your boss or leader. Instead of getting frustrated at their imperfection, try praying for the leaders around you. Leading isn't easy, and I'm sure they could use all the prayer they can get.

And if you are the leader of your church, business, school, or team, then let's attempt to learn from others' mistakes so you can become the best boss you can possibly be!

ONE

SAUL:
THE INSECURE BOSS

"YOU ARE ALWAYS AT YOUR BEST WHEN YOU ARE THE MOST REAL YOU."

Dan Reiland, The Pastor's Coach

Of all the negative character traits a boss could have, perhaps the worst is insecurity. Insecure leaders are full of self-doubt and jealousy, which usually results in their organization constantly operating on pins and needles. Those who follow insecure leaders are left to wonder how they can satisfy someone who is never truly satisfied with themselves.

If you're leading a church, team, school, or business, please remember that God has called you to be you. You are never more creative or original than when you are comfortable in your own skin. Posers and pretenders don't last long, and no one enjoys their company. And not only does no one enjoy being around an insecure leader, but they also don't want to run through a wall for one either. Calm, self-confidence is a leadership trait that others want to follow.

Insecure leaders require all the credit for the success and share in none of the blame for the failures. If that's you, you have a serious shelf life to your leadership. Furthermore, your organization has some severe limitations to its future.

In the Bible, we find a leader that fits that very description. His name is Saul - we talked about him briefly in the introduction. After the Israelites gave up on God being their primary ruler, Saul became their first king. It's safe to say he had some pretty big shoes to fill! And while he had a great start to his leadership, he suffered a terribly sad ending. We could aptly describe Saul as the Insecure Boss.

What do we know about Saul? Let's take a look at three of his major traits:

#1 - Tall

First of all, we know that Saul was tall. That's a great thing to be, I suppose. Not that I would know!

There was an influential man of Benjamin named Kish, son of Abiel, son of Zeror, son of Becorath, son of Aphiah, son of the Benjaminite. He had a son named Saul, an impressive young man. There was no one more impressive among the Israelites than he. He stood a head taller than anyone else. (1 Samuel 9:1-2)

Saul was tall, dark, and handsome on the outside. Yet as we study his life in more detail, we're going to discover that he was actually tall, broody, and unstable on the inside. He was insanely jealous and insecure.

Have you ever noticed that it's usually the best looking and most gifted people who are often the most insecure? It's odd, isn't it? I mean, sometimes I just thank God that he made me short, fat, and ugly. When you're short, fat, and ugly - you think you can rule the world!

But many times, it is the most handsome, beautiful, and outstandingly gifted who think very little of themselves. The Hollywood crowd is a great case study in this. So much of a celebrity's identity and self-worth can be attached to appearance instead of who they are inside.

We need to be careful not to assume that just because someone looks like Saul on the outside, they have a heart of a David on the inside. Often times appearances can be misleading.

#2 - Talented

Not only was Saul tall, but we also find that he was talented.

When Saul turned around to leave Samuel, God changed his heart, and all the signs came about that day. When Saul and his attendant arrived at Gibeah, a group of prophets met him. Then the Spirit of God took control of him, and he prophesied along with them."

Everyone who knew him previously and saw him prophesy with the prophets asked each other, "What has happened to the son of Kish? Is Saul also among the prophets?"

Then a man who was from there asked, "And who is their father?"

As a result, "Is Saul also among the prophets?" became a popular saying. (1 Samuel 10:9-12)

For all of Saul's weaknesses, there was a degree of

greatness in him. He was introduced back in 1 Samuel 9 as "impressive." And the Scripture not only called him that once but twice! We see in 1 Samuel 10 that the spirit of God "took control of him" and used him to prophesy.

Later, Saul would lead Israel to many victorious battles. The people of that day chanted, "Saul has killed his thousands, but David his tens of thousands." (1 Samuel 18:7) David may have led Israel's army to kill more men than Saul, but Saul still killed his thousands. He had been a significant wartime king. He experienced more success than most of us have seen in our lifetimes.

Not only was Saul tall, but he was also talented.

#3 - Temperamental

Saul did have an Achilles heel, and it was that he was very temperamental. Check out his jealousy:

As the troops were coming back, when David was returning from killing the Philistine, the women came out from all the cities of Israel to meet King Saul, singing and dancing with tambourines, with shouts of joy, and with three-stringed instruments. As they celebrated, the women sang:

"Saul has killed his thousands,
but David his tens of thousands."

Saul was furious and resented this song. "They credited tens of thousands to David," he complained, "but they only credited me with thousands. What more can he have but the kingdom?" So Saul watched David jealously from that day forward. (1 Samuel 18:6-9)

Saul should have been ecstatic that his apprentice David was growing into his own shoes as a leader. The more successful David became, the more successful Israel would be. But insecurity doesn't allow you to celebrate others, only yourself. So Saul watched David jealously from that day forward.

The Bible tells us that the next day an evil spirit sent from God took control of Saul, and he began to rave inside the palace. And that same thing would happen over and over again. Saul had fits of turmoil, rage, and despair consistently. So, Saul would bring David in to play the harp, attempting to soothe the king's soul.

David was Saul's confidant, a compliment to his leadership, and even cared deeply for him. Yet while David played the harp, Saul would hold his spear while the anger inside of him grew. Once he felt jealous and insecure enough, he would hurl it at David, trying to kill him.

Now that is what you call an unhealthy workplace environment! If you go to a staff meeting and the boss is throwing spears at you, it's safe to say it might be time to look for another job. At the very least, that's something you should report to Human Resources!

What in the world happened? Saul began to see David, a valuable resource in his kingdom, as a threat. If you were the king and had a general killing tens-of-thousands of your enemies, that's a good thing! Can we agree on that? Nonetheless, he began to see David as a threat, rather than an asset, to his leadership. He became fixated on David and became insanely jealous of him.

THE EFFECTS OF ATTITUDE

How often does that happen in workplaces? How about on leadership teams? When the boss isn't comfortable in their own skin, they will begin to see rising stars in the organization as liabilities instead of the assets they truly are.

A tranquil heart is life to the body, but jealousy is rottenness to the bones. (Proverbs 14:30)

"Fury is cruel, and anger is a flood, but who can withstand jealousy?" (Proverbs 27:4)

It's a great question, isn't it? Who can withstand jealousy? The answer is no relationship, no workplace, no sports team, and no political platform can withstand jealousy. It is a cancer that eats away at your job, relationships, team, or life. And the only way to deal with cancer is by having it removed.

When insecurity and jealousy aren't dealt with, the results can be disastrous. Of all the traits we will see in these bad bosses of the Bible throughout this book, the absolute worst is insecurity.

When you work for an insecure boss, you always have to walk on eggshells, affirm the leader, and support their ego. Staff meetings become a mutual admiration society for the boss. Over the long haul, this results in a caustic, unhealthy environment where those around the leader intuitively know they can't trust them with their hearts. Who knows when they might start flinging spears your way!

THE ATTITUDE OF THE LEADER WILL GREATLY AFFECT THE HEALTH OF THE ORGANIZATION.

The attitude of the boss, or leader, will greatly affect the health of the organization. A leader with a healthy view of themselves will produce a healthy and happy team.

When the leader is secure, then you will find that a great majority of the affirmation and the encouragement flows down the leadership pipeline instead of up. The boss becomes the source of positive words, affirmation, and encouragement - the way it should be.

In an unhealthy work relationship, it is just the opposite. By design of the boss, most encouragement and affirmation travel up the leadership pipeline instead of down. The employees end up with the job of telling the boss how great and glorious they are. That is unhealthy!

Some of you are reading this and thinking, *Well, I'm the boss. I deserve some credit. I deserve some affirmation.* True! You deserve *some*. And the more selflessly you lead, the more you will naturally get. But get this: because you get paid the most, you deserve affirmation the least. Your big benefit is you get the biggest check. You also might get the most headaches and responsibilities. That's the reality of those who say yes to leadership. Still, it would be beneficial for you and your team if you didn't feel like you deserved the most credit out of everyone. It's not that affirmation isn't important. But as the leader, the bulk of your encouragement should come from peers outside of your team or organization.

Your number one job as a boss is to celebrate the successes of others! Saul should have celebrated David's wins, but instead, he resented them. It ended up not only hurting their relationship but also weakening the entire nation of Israel.

Celebrating those around you is the glue that holds people and teams together. It's also what helps defeat insecurity inside of you. If you're in a relationship, you should celebrate your partner's successes even more so than your own. If you're on a team, you should cheer on your teammates enthusiastically. If you're in the workplace, you should recognize when others perform well. If you're a boss, you should give all of the credit to those you lead.

I love this definition of a friend: someone who goes on loving you no matter how successful either of you become. I think it would be good for us to apply that definition to all of our relationships. That type of mentality encourages us to celebrate others instead of always trying to one-up each other.

If somebody at your work gets promoted, you should celebrate them. If someone else gets a raise, express how happy you are for them. If a co-worker gets some attaboys, give them one more. The worst thing you can do is to resent it, become jealous, and fixate on it.

GOD CHOSE YOU!

But what do you do if you're having a hard time, like Saul, with jealousy and insecurity? Regardless of how hard we try, we're all sinners who struggle. Some of us are going to have a more challenging time with insecurity than others. And maybe this is one of those deals that you have a tough time with. What are you supposed to do if you just can't shake insecurity and jealousy?

From a spiritual point of view, I believe the key is wrapped up in our understanding of who we are in Christ.

Often the Apostle Paul, in the New Testament, would introduce his letter to a local church by addressing their identity.

To the faithful saints in Christ Jesus at Ephesus... (Ephesians 1:1)

To the saints in Christ at Colossae... (Colossians 1:1)

We all have both a geographical location and a spiritual location. To some of the early churches Paul wrote to, Ephesus or Colossae were their geographical locations. Your geographical location might be at the church office, school, workplace, Honeywell, or Haliburton during the week. However, your spiritual location is more important to your self-confidence and self-worth.

Spiritually you are located "in Christ," and that's the most important thing about you! That's why in Paul's letters, he addresses spiritual location before geographical location. Before you're defined by anything else, you are called, loved, and chosen.

What a blessing it would have been for Saul to see that about himself. It would've been a game-changer to both him and those he led. And just as God had called Saul, he has called you and placed you in your current position of leadership. That thought alone should drive self-doubt and insecurity away. I'm convinced that the single most important way of overcoming jealousy and insecurity is understanding who you are in Christ.

Perry Noble writes, "Being in ministry for more than twenty years now has opened my eyes to the reality that people's lives on either side of the cross are messy. The difference is that those of us who are in Christ can move past the mess if we understand that our mess doesn't disqualify us for His love. If we ever lose sight of that, we will find ourselves constantly gathering around the religious latrine, celebrating our own performance and neglecting to celebrate the goodness of God." [1]

Wow! What a difference a self-confident leader makes in an organization. A leader who understands who they are in Christ can love, live, and lead out of the overflow of that understanding.

Unfortunately, many of us live as slaves to this false perception: we don't see ourselves as God does. Would it have changed Saul's outlook if he could have just seen himself as the chosen King of Israel? The people didn't vote on him - it wasn't a lottery system. They could have picked anyone they wanted, and yet God said, "choose Saul." Saul was so valuable to God that he was elevated above every other potential candidate. If he could have just seen himself as God did - worthy of kingship - it would have changed the trajectory of his entire identity. But like Saul, many of us live as slaves to our own perception that lies to us about who we really are.

A great example of faulty perception is found from a classic experiment which was first conducted in 1873 by a German zoologist named Dr. Karl Mobius. Dr. Mobius put a large pike in a tank of water and fed the pike small bait fish. After a while, he divided the tank by inserting a heavy pane of glass in it. Then, he dropped the small bait fish into the section separated from the pike by the glass.

The pike—an aggressive, voracious eater—charged the little fish. It charged over and over, and each time the pike charged into the fish to eat them, it crashed violently into the pane of glass. Sometimes it was so stunned by the impact that it floated upside down for a few minutes before recovering its senses. After several painful attempts, the pike gave up and no longer tried to get at the bait fish.

When Dr. Mobius removed the pane of glass, the pike and its prey peacefully shared the tank. The pike learned that pursuing the prey caused severe headaches. From then on, it would only eat food given to it by Dr. Mobius.

Researchers in the U.S. and Canada have repeated Mobius's experiment with the same results. Some have actually allowed the pike to starve to death, even as minnows swam around it and bumped into its head and mouth.

Reluctant and fearful behavior based on false assumptions has since become known as *Pike Syndrome*.[2]

I wonder how many of us sometimes lead with *Pike Syndrome*? It's easy to allow self-limiting beliefs, past failures, or perceived shortcomings to hold us back from new efforts. If you've been beaten up enough times, invisible barriers can start shaping your behaviors. But as a leader, if you are a believer in Jesus, then that means that you are in Christ. You are so much more valuable than what you perceive. You've been chosen by Jesus himself, and he's changed everything for you.

Mark it down - we have inexhaustible supplies for every need. They come from Jesus himself - the God of the universe who appointed you to the position you're currently in. That means that as a boss, you have all the love, patience, courage, wisdom, and faith you need through Christ.

Insecurity is nothing more than a false perception of yourself based on past issues. If you're struggling with it, try asking God to help you see yourself in Christ.

What if Saul would've done this? What if he could have celebrated David's success? I wish he could have had the self-confidence to have said: "David, before God even chose you, he chose me. I am his chosen king."

What if you could really see yourself the way God does? You wouldn't visualize somebody that's just run of the mill. Yes, you'd see a boss or a leader. But more than that, you'd see yourself as a boss or leader who is first and foremost a child of God. You were chosen by him before the foundations of the world. Your spiritual location is in

Christ.

So, if you're struggling with jealousy and insecurity - can I give you some advice? Stop it! Stop worrying if you're in the cool crowd. Stop concerning yourself with what others think about you. Stop comparing your success to the accolades and accomplishments of others. Live your life for the approval and audience of one person, Jesus Christ. Understand that you are accepted in the Beloved. Build your identity based upon who you are in Christ, and watch as jealousy and insecurity become a thing of the past.

CELEBRATING OTHERS' SUCCESS

Here is a tell-tale sign that you've reached an understanding of your true identity: you will celebrate, not resent, the accomplishments of others around you. Unfortunately, Saul never learned that lesson. Instead of cheering for David, he was jealous of him. And his resentment continued to grow until it was a raging torrent that couldn't be controlled.

GOOD BOSS TAKEAWAY:

GOOD LEADERS AREN'T THREATENED BY THE SUCCESS OF OTHERS, THEY CELEBRATE IT.

What would happen if you took that one simple principle to work with you tomorrow and applied it? What would happen to your church staff? On your team? In your office? If you could take this one little nugget back to those you lead, it might change the entire culture, climate, and environment around what you do. The best leaders celebrate the success of those they lead instead of resenting it.

As a leader, when you create a culture of celebration, it will inevitably bring you great joy. The act of celebration is contagious. When a leader celebrates their followers, their followers start to celebrate the leader, their peers, and the organization in response. And when somebody celebrates the successes of those you lead, they are praising you by extension!

In the organization I lead, Cross Church, I will sometimes hear people bragging about our team. They'll talk about what a great job our worship pastor is doing, how thankful they are for our children's pastor, or how much they love one of our campus pastors. And I always love that and take it as a compliment. I smile on the inside because I know I'm the one who hired them! When those you lead are successful and celebrated, you are also being celebrated, and your leadership ability is rewarded.

So take this nugget to work with you tomorrow: Make it a point to celebrate those around you. Although it does take intentionality, it's not overly difficult!

As a leader, you'll earn the respect of those you lead. But you will also see the high tide of positivity rise across your entire team. When I celebrate the successes in our organization, I've learned it raises the bar for everyone.

Years ago, my friend and Executive Coach, Chris Sonksen, told me, "We get what we celebrate!" I have found that to be over the top true. Celebrating others helps you to become a secure leader who is comfortable in your own skin and confident in who you are in Christ. And when you celebrate, the entire organization will become more successful. That is the definition of a win-win!

GOOD BOSS REFLECTION + APPLICATION

Are people afraid to mess up around you? If you aren't sure, do the tough work of asking those that you lead. Their answer will reveal a lot about your leadership and organizational attitude.

What are your biggest insecurities and how do they affect others? Invite God into them and pray for help seeing yourself the way he already sees you.

How could you better celebrate those around you to boost morale at your workplace, in your marriage, with your kids, or amongst your friends?

DAVID:
THE FALLEN BOSS

HOW THE MIGHTY HAVE FALLEN AND THE WEAPONS OF WAR HAVE PERISHED!

1 Samuel 1:27

Here's a harsh truth that we don't like to think about: sometimes the best bosses can make the biggest mistakes. Just because you are a great leader or a great boss doesn't mean you can't or won't make a mistake. Likewise, your boss might be one of the best in the business. But regardless of how great they are, they'll also make a lot of mistakes! The reality is, we're all made of flesh and blood, and we all have the inevitable potential to get it wrong. Some of those mistakes might be marginal: mathematical errors and strategical blunders. Still, some of them may be much deeper and more destructive. Moral failures and moral disappointments can plague even the best of leaders.

Think of David, for example. He took the throne right after Saul and was opposite of him in almost every way. The Bible says that he was a man after God's own heart and as we study his life, we also see that he was an outstanding leader. He was one of the best bosses that the nation of Israel ever had. Because of his likable qualities, people were actually excited and committed to following him. And yet, when we look at the life of David, the thing we often remember the most was his moral failure. He committed adultery against his wife with a woman by the name of Bathsheba. Subsequently, he covered up the affair by orchestrating the murder of Bathsheba's husband, Uriah.

How could this be? How could such a great leader

have such a significant fall? The reality is that even the best bosses, the most remarkable leaders, can have huge successes but also make huge mistakes.

Fortunately for us, we can learn from the mistakes of leaders like David, so we don't have to suffer the consequences ourselves.

PROMISE

But the Lord said to Samuel, "Do not look at his appearance or his stature, because I have rejected him. Man does not see what the Lord sees, for man sees what is visible, but the Lord sees the heart." (1 Samuel 16:7)

After Jesse presented seven of his sons to him, Samuel told Jesse, "The Lord hasn't chosen any of these." Samuel asked him, "Are these all the sons you have?"

"There is still the youngest," he answered, "but right now he's tending the sheep." Samuel told Jesse, "Send for him. We won't sit down to eat until he gets here." So Jesse sent for him. He had beautiful eyes and a healthy, handsome appearance.

Then the Lord said, "Anoint him, for he is the one." (1 Samuel 16:10-12)

Let's start at the beginning with David. David starts off with great promise. He was the youngest of the sons of his father, Jesse. And the Bible tells us that Samuel, God's prophet, came to Jesse's house directed by the Lord to anoint a new king that would succeed Saul and lead the nation of Israel. And so, Jesse brought his sons to meet Samuel one-by-one. The only son that he failed to bring into Samuel's presence was the youngest, David. Because he was the youngest, Jesse probably didn't think David had any chance of being selected as Israel's next king. Samuel looked at each of the older boys and said, "No, this isn't the right guy. Definitely not him! Nope, he isn't the one."

Eventually, there were no sons left. Samuel was puzzled because the Lord had directed him to Jesse's home to find the next king. He asked Jesse if there was anybody else. And almost as an afterthought, Jesse said, "Oh yeah, there's still my youngest son, David." And so, Jesse fetched David. And when Samuel saw him, he knew that he was God's appointed future king. And this future king would turn out to be one of the best bosses ever.

We learn some things from Samuel's selection of David regarding what it takes to be a great leader:

#1 - Great leaders don't always make sense according to human reason.

Sometimes it just doesn't make sense. "This guy? Really? Are you choosing him?" And yet, human reason doesn't always line up with God's plan of who will be the best boss, leader, pastor, or coach. Just because it doesn't make sense to you doesn't mean it's not God!

#2 - Great leaders are identified by their hearts.

When Samuel looked at young David, he looked beyond the veneer and deeper than the surface. He saw something in his heart. It's no accident that the Bible says that David was a man after God's own heart (Acts 13:22). David had the right heart for leadership.

We give leaders a lot of credit for their smarts. And while it's true that leaders must have the right head, they must also have the right heart. They must let that heart guide them - not only in their relationship with God but also in their relationship with others. They need to have a heart for those that they lead. A sincere concern for those they have been providentially placed over is crucial to long-term leadership success. When your heart is healthy, you will want the best for your team and organization. To be a great leader, you must have the right heart.

#3 - Great leaders are appointed by heaven.

God's hand was clearly on David. Samuel, being a prophet, acted on God's behalf in appointing David. Therefore, David was chosen by God himself.

Leadership can often feel unbearable. There are hard times, lonely times, and times of isolation. During those times, the one thing that will get you through is the confidence that God has appointed you to your position.

We usually use words like *appointed* to describe pastoral positions. But I sincerely believe that all leaders are appointed. You have been called to lead your business. And the people at your business are dependent upon you to lead well. You've been called to be the administrator at your local school. And the children and parents depend upon you to lead well. You've been placed in your position!

The Bible even talks about God appointing politicians and kings to their positions of authority. That means that God is heavily involved in leadership selection! We may think that we orchestrate or manipulate the process to obtain leadership, but in the end, God has allowed you to be where you're at. And when the dark nights of leadership come, it is incredibly important to know that God has called you.

It seems as if David understood this, and therefore started really well. I mean, he began like a horse bolting out of the Kentucky Derby gate. He ran really fast and really well. He was a young leader with great promise and potential.

COURAGE

"Your servant has killed lions and bears; this uncircumcised Philistine will be like one of them, for he has defied the armies of the living God." (1 Samuel 17:36)

Not only did David have promise, but he also had courage. As David continued to grow, he continued to have success. He killed a lion and a bear, which gave him confidence that he could ultimately face down a giant when he came across him.

You probably know the famous story of David and Goliath. While he was still a shepherd, David went to the Israelite war camp as they were in a fierce battle against the Philistines. His brothers were seasoned warriors, and David went to resupply them with resources they might need. When David arrived, he saw that his brothers, and all the other seasoned warriors, were cowering in fear over a Philistine giant named Goliath. And to make matters worse, David heard Goliath taunting God's army.

When David witnessed all of this, passion boiled up on the inside of him. He questioned why God's chosen warriors were so afraid. Even though he was only a shepherd, he essentially said, "I can take him. God's with me. If nobody else is willing, I'll do it myself." He went to the leader of Israel's army, Saul, and said, "Listen, let me have a shot at this giant."

While the rest of the world thought Goliath was too big to hit, David thought he was too big to miss.

Armed with only a sling and a stone, David strutted onto the battlefield to meet Goliath. While he was a shepherd, God had helped him defeat lions and bears to protect his sheep. He was confident that the same God who helped him kill vicious animals would help him defeat Goliath. He whipped that sling above his head and released the stone. He flung it forward with the precision, accuracy, and force of a bullet fired from a Colt 45. And it struck Goliath right between the eyes. *Bam!* The giant fell over dead. But David didn't stop there. He took a sword, cut the head of Goliath off, and brought it back as a trophy to the tent of the Israelites. Goliath's big old melon-head was proof that God brought Israel's army victory. But it happened because of the extraordinary courage of a young man named David.

It takes great courage to lead an organization. For

leaders to lead their people to victory, they must walk on the edge and do things others wouldn't. Leadership is synonymous with risk.

David isn't the only example we see in the Old Testament. Later on, God called Joshua to lead Israel across the Jordan River and into the Promised Land. He repeatedly reminded Joshua of his commissioning and the courage of a leader. God challenged him, "Be strong and courageous, for you will distribute the land I swore to their fathers to give them as an inheritance." (Joshua 1:6) And He reminded him again just a few verses later: "Haven't I commanded you: to be strong and *courageous?*" (Joshua 1:9)

Why did God repeat himself? Because leaders need courage!

Another excellent example of courageous leadership is a lady named Esther. Before she asked for a favor from the king, which could have costed her life, she said, "...If I perish, I perish." (Esther 4:16) What courage we see in this great leader!

I can't emphasize this enough: leadership requires courage. You will have to make decisions, step out in faith, and do things that others are reluctant to do. Why? Simply because you are the leader.

Just remember, leaders are like pioneers who often got attacked by arrows flying just over their heads. The same reality is true for you. Leaders must have the courage to face the Goliaths of the world, cross the Jordan River when it's flooding, and go into the court of the king when their life is on the line. In your organization, it might play out a little differently. You might need the courage to invest in that big project, change your staff culture, or make risky decisions! Nonetheless, great courage is required for great leadership.

LOYALTY

Another thing about David, which is also true of great leaders, is that he was a man of loyalty. Even after being anointed as the next king of Israel, he continued to serve under the current king, Saul. You remember Saul - an insanely jealous and insecure leader? On multiple occasions, Saul tried to kill David. He threw his own sword at him, trying to eliminate the threat he falsely perceived him to be. Because people were simply giving David the credit he was due, Saul's jealousy wanted him dead. But despite that, David still remained loyal to Saul.

I think one of the most impressive characteristics of great leadership is deep loyalty. David was willing to wait for his turn and support his boss, even though he was arguably more accomplished. David understood something completely lost in our society today. If you want to be a person of authority, you must first be a person under authority. Jesus himself said as much. The truth is, if you're too big to take orders, you'll never be big enough to give orders. That's important to remember!

And so, David had all of these wonderful attributes. He had promise, courage, and loyalty. But this is where the worm turns.

IF YOU ARE TOO BIG TO TAKE ORDERS THEN YOU WILL NEVER BE BIG ENOUGH TO GIVE ORDERS.

BLIND SPOT

In the spring when kings march out to war, David sent Joab with his officers and all Israel. They destroyed the Ammonites and besieged Rabbah, but David remained in Jerusalem.

One evening David got up from his bed and strolled around on the roof of the palace. From the roof he saw a woman bathing—a very beautiful woman. So David sent someone to inquire about her, and he reported, "This is Bathsheba, daughter of Eliam and wife of Uriah the Hittite."

David sent messengers to get her, and when she came to him, he slept with her. (2 Samuel 11:1-4)

David had a blind spot. At the time of year when kings went off to war, he stayed home. Instead of fulfilling his leadership responsibilities, he remained at his palace. And one day, with nothing to preoccupy him, David observed a woman bathing on a nearby rooftop. He began to lust after her and eventually invited her up to his place. Even though she was married, he committed adultery with the woman named Bathsheba- the bathing beauty.

Eventually, Bathsheba became pregnant. Her baby bump became obvious evidence of her and David's sinful behavior. So, David tried to cover it up. Uriah, Bathsheba's husband, was a soldier in David's army and therefore under his command. He brought him back home from the battlefield and encouraged him to sleep with his wife. But Uriah didn't feel good about enjoying his wife while his fellow soldiers were still on the battlefield. So instead of sleeping with Bathsheba, he slept outside.

Uriah was a man of integrity, just like David had once been. And as a result of that, eventually, David's sin found him out. Nathan, the prophet, came and confronted David.

There was a huge blind spot in David's life. He was in the wrong place at the wrong time and used his success to take selfish liberties. He sent others to lead his troops when he should have been at war. And in isolation, while others were away, David thought it was time to play.

Blind spots - we all have them! They are areas that cause us to be vulnerable that we just can't see.

A couple of years ago, we bought my wife a Kia Optima. Overall it's been a very quality car, but I noticed early on that it has one major flaw. The way that the mirrors are positioned results in poor visibility for the driver. It creates a real blind spot just near the rear quarter panel.

When I first started driving it, I inadvertently pulled

into oncoming traffic several times because I couldn't see the cars coming from behind. But now that we've figured it out, we take extra precautions before changing lanes. Especially when we're moving from the right lane to the left lane because we know that's where the blind spot is.

Blind spots don't have to be terminal for leaders. If we know we have them, we can put precautions in place to deal with them. If we can say, "Hey, listen, I've got a little weakness here," then others can help us add some extra support in that area.

At the start of this chapter, we talked about how the best bosses can make the biggest mistakes. That's because they have blind spots. Every leader has traits that if they don't take extra precautions to guard, they will naturally lead to failure over time. That's regardless of how good and gifted they are!

GOOD BOSS TAKEAWAY:

THE VERY THINGS THAT MAKE LEADERS CAN ALSO BREAK LEADERS.

The very things that make leaders can also break leaders. Think about it. Leaders, by nature, are risk-takers. They need to be people of courage and passion who are willing to step out and do bold things! Those qualities are what make them leaders.

But the same qualities that will make you a great

leader can also make you very vulnerable when it comes to your blind spots. They can cause you to be intrigued by risky behavior. The courage that makes you a great leader can also allure you to act out. It can serve as fuel for those activities that, in the end, may take you down. When we allow our blind spot to take over and make major mistakes, it affects others as well - in our families, businesses, schools, and churches.

The book, *When a Leader Falls*, tells the story of a pastor named Jim who suffered a moral failure. Here's what it says: "When Jim chose to fall (and yes, it was his choice; sin is always a choice), everyone around him fell as well – his wife, their children, the relatives, the church leaders, the congregation, his past congregation, friends and acquaintances, the community. Their falls were different from his; they did not fall into sin. Some fell into disillusionment and some into distrust and anger. Others fell into rationalization of their own immoral behavior – gossip, hate, or even a loss of faith. One after another they all fell down the hill and into the heap."[1]

Like Jim, David's failure affected others. It ended up resulting in a divided kingdom as Judah and Israel split ways. A man and a baby would both die. Terrible things happened in the wake of David's failure, not just in his life, but also in the lives of those he was called to lead.

We need to understand that the potential effects of a leadership fall on the organization we lead can be catastrophic.

So how do we safeguard our lives from failure, mistakes, and blind spots? The answer lies in building guardrails!

BUILDING GUARDRAILS

Recently, my wife and I went on a vacation to Colorado. Because we love the mountains so much it's become our new favorite place. On this particular trip, we met some friends and spent a week riding bikes in the Rocky Mountains. We both rode our Harley's to Telluride. From there, we rode around on the Million Dollar Highway - the famous stretch of road that takes you from Durango to Silverton and even further up to Ouray. The ride includes some of the most beautiful scenery anywhere in the world. I even saw my first ever wild moose on the route.

But when you ride your motorcycle on the Million Dollar Highway, you have to pay close attention. Even with the beautiful scenery, you have little time to look at mountains, moose, or picture-perfect sunsets. Navigating the switch-backs, sharp curves, and steep cliffs demands intense focus.

For the most part, the most scenic parts of the ride have the steepest cliffs - which, of course, don't have any guardrails. The highway is so narrow that there's not even room for them. It makes for a breathtaking, extremely dangerous ride through the mountains.

The ride reminds me of the way we sometimes navigate life and leadership. Steep cliffs and no guardrails! Some of us produce some beautiful things but also operate on the edge of danger. Let's talk about some of the most necessary guardrails to put in place so we can protect our leadership and personal lives.

Guardrail #1 - Self-leadership

Oscar Wilde, author and playwright, was one who paid scant attention to his private life. Wilde once made this confession:

"The gods had given me almost everything. But I let myself be lured into long spells of senseless and sensual ease... Tired of being on the heights, I deliberately went into the depths in search for new sensation. What the paradox was to be in the sphere of thought, perversity became to me the sphere of passion. I grew careless of the lives of others. I took pleasure where it pleased me and passed on. I forgot that every little action of the common day makes or unmakes character, and that therefore what one has done in the secret chamber, one has some day to cry aloud from the house-top. I ceased to be lord over myself. I was no longer the captain of my soul and did not know it. I allowed pleasure to dominate me. I ended in horrible disgrace."[2]

Did you hear that? He was no longer the captain of his own soul. The first guardrail you need to build into the highway of your life is self-leadership. To be a great leader, for a long time, you first must learn to lead yourself. Ironically, the hardest person you will ever lead is yourself. But until you can lead yourself well, you won't be able to lead others well. Leaders are readers, growers, developers, and learners.

I love Gordon MacDonald's personal checklist of things that prevent him from leading himself well:

- I'm living at too fast a speed.
- I am awash in too many choices, and I'm not good at saying no.
- I'm overwhelmed by the complexities of my organization.
- I compare myself to other people... and I always feel like I lose.
- I think that technology and talent can solve my problems, but they can't.
- I am tempted to think that all I have to do is preach to people and they will come around.
- I have not respected the fore of the anti-faith culture I'm living in.
- I am not seeking times of deep reverence, prayer, and the presence of Jesus.[3]

Guardrail #2 - Sexual Purity

A second guardrail you will need is one that will protect you from sexual impurity. And for those that think you could never fall in this area, I refer you back to King David, a man after God's own heart. If you feel sexual perversion is impossible for you, you may be flirting with a blind spot.

I love this point by Dr. David Jeremiah: "If sexual purity isn't a problem, you are more godly than David; stronger than Samson; and wiser than Solomon."[4]

Recognizing the potential for failure, the late great Billy Graham built a guardrail into his life to protect from sexual impurity. In 1948 at the beginning of his ministry, Billy and his team penned what became known as the Modesto Manifesto.

"The second item on the list was the danger of sexual immorality. We all knew of evangelists who had fallen into immorality while separated from their families by travel. We pledged among ourselves to avoid any situation that would have even the appearance of compromise or suspicion. From that day on, I did not travel, meet, or eat alone with a woman other than my wife. We determined that the Apostle Paul's mandate to the young pastor Timothy would be ours as well: 'Flee ... youthful lusts' (2 Timothy 1:22, KJV)."[5]

While in office, Vice President Mike Pence made headlines by declaring he personally practices the Modesto Manifesto's second tenant. This is wisdom not just for Pence and Graham, but for all of us as leaders.

Guardrail #3 - Accountability

Thirdly, one of the most important guardrails leaders can build into their lives to keep from those steep cliffs is accountability. I implore you, don't be a lone ranger. Be accountable to your spouse, team, friends, and others. Make accountability a part of your personal DNA. If David had been accountable with his time, he would have been with his soldiers, not alone in his palace. Everything changes when you're one-hundred percent accountable to those that you are called to lead.

In the end, guardrails defend us against our greatest enemy - ourselves. Over the years, I have seen too many gifted leaders fall even though they seemingly looked like they had it all. Good looks, sharp minds, and exceptional people skills didn't prevent them from biting the dust.

Why? Because some of the same traits that make a leader, if left unchecked, can break a leader.

OWN IT!

Here's an important question: what happens if you do mess up? What happens if you career over the rail and fall down the steep cliff? If, or when, this happens, you need to do exactly what David did. He painted a powerful and productive picture of what we should do when we fall over the cliff.

I mean, nobody fell over a steeper cliff than King David. We can learn not only from his mistake but also from his response to that mistake. How did he respond? He owned it. I wish I could shout this to make sure you hear it loud and clear: HE OWNED IT!

David owned his mistake and repented of it. Listen to his response once he was confronted with his sin:

Be gracious to me, God,
according to Your faithful love;
according to Your abundant compassion,
blot out my rebellion.
Wash away my guilt
and cleanse me from my sin.
For I am conscious of my rebellion,
and my sin is always before me.
Against You—You alone—I have sinned
and done this evil in Your sight.
So You are right when You pass sentence;
You are blameless when You judge. (Psalms 51:1-4)

When you read Psalms 51, you see all of the personal pronouns that David used. He didn't play the blame game. He took personal responsibility.

During the Coronavirus pandemic, the Speaker of the House, Nancy Pelosi, was caught getting her hair washed and blow-dried in a San Francisco salon. It doesn't sound like a big deal, and it probably wasn't. But it made national news because California was in the middle of a statewide lockdown. There was a rule that said you couldn't get your hair done in a local salon. Maybe a silly rule to some, but still a rule, nonetheless. And so, she got caught. Not a failure as extreme as David's, but still a failure according to governmental regulations.

The following day, she talked about how she was set up, and it was somebody else's fault. And get this - she only took responsibility for allowing herself to be set up!

That's not the kind of ownership we see from David. It's not the type of ownership we should see from any type of leader. When we're caught, do we have the personal integrity to own it? We should have the courage to say, "I did this. It's nobody else's fault but my own." That's what David did. And it gives a blueprint for us to follow when we fail.

The best thing a leader can do is admit when he or she is wrong. It might be a massive moral failure, or it might be something seemingly insignificant. Either way, ownership important! It can be as simple as: "I treated you poorly, and I'm sorry. I was wrong. I was dismissive of your idea, and I'm sorry. I was wrong." Great leaders know that apologies must complement authority. Otherwise, authority is quickly misunderstood as abusive. Forgiveness is foundational in every relationship, organization, or corporation.

Because David owned his mistake, God did not disown him. God continued to call David a man after his own heart. David's affair was not right by any means, but God still believed in him even after failure. After David took ownership of his fall, God's hand was there to help him back up.

Maybe you are on the backside of a mistake or moral failure. The good news is that what was said of David can be said of you. There is still a future and hope for you. But first, you must own it. You have to stop making excuses and ask for forgiveness.

Remember, even the best excuses are still excuses. In fact, an excuse is just the skin of a reason stuffed full of a lie.

So, please stop making excuses. Stop coming up with alibis. Be big enough to admit it when you are wrong and watch both God and others find a new-found respect for you as a leader.

And what if you've been affected by the bad choices of a boss or a leader? What if you're on the receiving end of that request for forgiveness? I would simply say that you need to be big enough to grant forgiveness when requested. We can't expect to receive forgiveness for our mistakes while being unwilling to extend forgiveness to our leaders. I love the words of one of America's leading theologians, the great football coach, Lou Holtz. He said, "People need forgiveness the most when they deserve it the least."[6]

Please don't be stingy with your forgiveness. Trust

me, one day you will need it yourself. The Bible says, "For whatever a man sows he will also reap..." (Galatians 6:7) If we sow stinginess in forgiveness, we'll reap a stingy, unforgiving culture. As a leader, you want to forgive, and in return, be able to receive forgiveness.

Every organization desperately needs to create a culture of ownership and forgiveness. David, a person of great promise, courage, and loyalty, had a massive blind spot. But when he fell, he owned it. And that's why he's probably the best of the bad bosses that we are studying. From him, we can learn that even the best of bosses can make big mistakes and operate as a bad boss for a season.

Maybe that's the season you're in now. But here's some good news - you don't have to live in that season forever. You can take ownership, ask for forgiveness, and make the remarkable turnaround of becoming a better boss, leader, and most importantly, person. Let's create a culture of second chances, together!

GOOD BOSS REFLECTION + APPLICATION

Are there any mistakes - big or small - that you've made as a leader? How have you worked on bouncing back from them?

Which guardrail do you think would be the most important to build into your life immediately: self-leadership, sexual purity, or accountability? Write down an action step you can take to ensure it gets built.

Ask God to reveal any blunders you need to receive forgiveness for. You may need to apologize to your spouse, kids, team, or boss. I bet you'll be shocked by the freedom and healing it brings!

THREE

ADONIJAH:
THE WANNABE BOSS

"CAUSE I SAID I WANNA BE A BOSS
I SAID I WANNA BE A BOSS
AND I'LL HAVE PEOPLE WORKIN' UNDER
ME AND THIS LOUSY JOB I'LL TOSS. I
SAID I WANNA BE A BOSS"

Stan Ridgway

Bad bosses are everywhere - secular offices, church offices, political offices, and sports franchises are filled with them. It was no different with the nation of Israel in the Old Testament. They experienced a litany of bad bosses. In the last chapter, we looked at one of their best bosses in David, who was a man after God's own heart. Yet even David's life was marked by mistakes and failures. His crowning act was that he was humble enough to admit his wrongs and apologize.

As we pick back up in Israel's leadership journey, David is about to die. Leading up to his death, Israel needed to appoint a new king. If we use our vernacular, it was time for them to hire a new boss.

It's important to remember that in some ways, David was a great king. In other ways, he was not so great. He was described as a man after God's own heart and genuinely tried to lead from the contents of that heart. But he also had a sordid affair with Bathsheba, resulting in a child out of wedlock that died shortly after birth. David even murdered Bathsheba's husband, Uriah, attempting to hide his sin in a moment of panic. It resulted in a divided kingdom.

That's the guy who shares God's heart? It's a great reminder about leadership. There is greatness but also sinfulness inside of all leaders. It's important to understand that.

David had been a successful wartime king for Israel. Yet, he recognized the next season would require a different type of leadership. Therefore, the successful wartime king appointed Solomon, who would be a successful peacetime king. But before Solomon officially stepped into power, we find David on his deathbed, unable to keep warm. An interesting cure was ordered for the old king.

Now King David was old and getting on in years. Although they covered him with bedclothes, he could not get warm. So his servants said to him: "Let us search for a young virgin for my lord the king. She is to attend the king and be his caregiver. She is to lie by your side so that my lord the king will get warm." They searched for a beautiful girl throughout the territory of Israel; they found Abishag the Shunammite and brought her to the king. The girl was of unsurpassed beauty, and she became the king's caregiver. She served him, but he was not intimate with her. (1 Kings 1:1-4)

I'm sorry, but I have a curious mind. "Why does the Bible go to such great lengths to give us all the details of this story? Was Abishag just a 900 BC electric blanket, or was there something more going on there? And if she was just the blanket, why did she have to be so darn beautiful? I mean, a 500-pounder would have kept David warmer, right?"

That's just how I think! Some stuff just makes you

say "hmmm." Obviously, there's a big question mark around Abishag, and we'll get back to her before this chapter is over. Make sure she doesn't get lost in your mind.

But while David was near death and staying warm with his new electric blanket, there was turmoil in the kingdom. There was a power-play going on just outside of his doors. It was fueled by a man named Adonijah. He was one of David's sons, not by the marriage of Bathsheba, but by a different woman. Even though the throne did not rightfully belong to Adonijah, he was about to claim his right to be the King of Israel.

I'm going to call Adonijah the wannabe boss.

Have you ever come across a wannabe boss? They are people who want to lead before it's their time. They forcefully push their way into positions of power. When leadership isn't given to them organically, they take it forcefully. That's a perfect description of Adonijah. But it wasn't totally his fault.

David had failed on one of the basics of leadership. Unfortunately, he didn't set forth a clear succession plan for when he was gone. This mistake should serve as a massive lesson for us.

GOOD BOSS TAKEAWAY:

GREAT LEADERS ALWAYS HAVE A SUCCESSION PLAN IN PLACE.

Suppose you lead an organization, business, church, team, or department. You need to be preparing and training the person who will take over your leadership. Great leaders always have a succession plan in place when they're gone. How you leave your organization is probably even more important than what you do while you're with the organization. Think about it. You could build a team, organization, or company that's really special. But if you walk away without a succession plan, all the years of hard work are going to be destroyed. The positive impact you made in people's lives might become a negative one.

While David was on his death bed, his son Adonijah made a power grab for the kingdom because there was no clear succession plan in place. There was only one problem for Adonijah; God had not anointed, nor had he appointed, him to be the king. He was a wannabe king, wannabe leader, and wannabe boss. The fallout from his presumptuous behavior was enormous. Eventually, Solomon was anointed king, and all of a sudden, Adonijah found himself on the wrong side of the story.

If you lead anyone who always tries to involve themselves in decisions above their pay grade, then this chapter is for you. On the flip side of the coin, if you've ever tried to pry your way into a position that you weren't ready for, this chapter is for you, as well. Suppose you're a young leader that has an unhealthy thirst for more influence and power. In that case, this is about to help you significantly. And if you have the important responsibility of appointing a new leader, you need to tune in!

In the story of Adonijah and Solomon, we see that

choosing the right boss is incredibly important but also very difficult.

One of the hardest parts of my job is hiring new leaders in our organization. It's unexpectedly challenging to discern who's ready for the next level of leadership and who's not. To me, firing is much easier than hiring. When you fire someone, you most likely had months or even years to evaluate their performance. When you're in the process of hiring someone, you only have a resume and brief interview to go from.

In large, this is why I'm convinced that whenever possible, it's best to train up leaders and promote from within. When you do so, you have more than a resume and an interview to inform an organization altering decision. You've had a long time to instill a culture and analyze results. Ultimately, it leads to a much better decision.

The selection of leadership is so crucial because they carry the most weight in setting an organization's culture and tone. Making an impact on people, whether positive or negative, is inevitable. The cost that organizations pay because of leaders' moral, financial, relational, and ego failures is enormous.

I understand that leaders sometimes get injured by those that they lead. But God's word speaks more about the price of failed leaders, false prophets, evil kings, money-grubbing bosses, and power-hungry priests. They get the bulk of Christ's condemnation in the Scriptures.

That's why choosing a leader is a huge, heavy decision. Bad leaders and poor decisions damage followers. Because David didn't make his choice clear, when it came time to choose a new leader, Israel was in a crosshair of a decision.

Adonijah decided to try to wrestle the leadership away for himself. Let's dive into what we know about Adonijah.

HE ASPIRED TO BE THE BOSS

First of all, Adonijah aspired to be the king.

Adonijah son of Haggith kept exalting himself, saying, "I will be king!" He prepared chariots, cavalry, and 50 men to run ahead of him. But his father had never once reprimanded him by saying, "Why do you act this way?" In addition, he was quite handsome and was born after Absalom. (1 Kings 1:5-6)

There's a lot to be learned from the biblical language uses to describe Adonijah's attitude. He continually exalted himself, proclaiming himself as the king. You must be careful with people who promote themselves and talk about how in charge they are, when they actually aren't. Adonijah had visions of grandeur. He arrogantly decided that the kingship was his to be had without consulting with God or anybody else. He viewed it as his right.

Adonijah had an extreme sense of entitlement.

Entitlement has been a catchphrase to describe the climate of upcoming leaders in our current culture. Unfortunately, I believe entitlement is about to hit the American workforce and church offices like a tsunami in the next several years. Kids raised with club sports, unlimited travel, and little restraint will be the leaders of churches and companies in the years to come. I have faith that many of them will shake off the shackles of childhood entitlement and become outstanding leaders. Unfortunately, others will simply translate childhood entitlement into a new form of adult entitlement. And adult entitlement, coupled with a degree of power, can be a dangerous mix.

What caused Adonijah's sense of adult entitlement?

First, he was never taught differently by his dad. It turns out that David, with all his positive character traits, was a passive father. It says in 1 Kings 1:6 that David "had never once reprimanded him by saying, 'Why do you act this way?'"

We live in a culture of unreprimanded young people entering the job force. And if you are older and reading this, don't get too puffed up. You raised them! It's not a new phenomenon. Even in the Old Testament, the entitlement that unreprimanded children carried was problematic.

Nevertheless, today we have a group of young people who think they are entitled to the corner office without paying their dues. And why wouldn't they? They grew up in a culture where everyone gets a trophy and orange slices after the game, regardless of the score. It's so important to teach your children and grandchildren the importance of authority. If you neglect this responsibility, don't be surprised when they look for shortcuts instead of waiting on God's perfect plan. We must seize the opportunity to stop replicating modern-day Adonijah attitudes!

There's a second thing that caused a sense of entitlement in Adonijah's life. 1 Kings 1:6 lets us know that Adonijah "was quite handsome."

He isn't the first handsome man associated with the

kingship of Israel. Do you remember the first king, Saul? He was tall, dark, and handsome and his looks on the outside turned out to not match his character on the inside.

Because of guys like Saul and Adonijah, I sometimes tell our church that I'm thankful to be short, fat, and ugly. On one such occasion, one of our retired pastors encouraged me after service by saying: "Preacher, you aren't fat at all!" I politely responded with a "thank you," only to realize later that afternoon that he was calling me ugly!

I don't know what it's like to be handsome, but Adonijah did and he had a sense of entitlement because of it. To make matters worse, he was the eldest living son. His only older brother, Absalom, had already died, which automatically promoted Adonijah to the position of the oldest child. Often times, the eldest children would inherit the most power. So in Adonijah's mind, his birth order gave him the right to be the man. It's a good boss takeaway that I don't want you to miss.

GOOD BOSS TAKEAWAY:

GOOD LOOKS
+
FAVORED STATUS
+
PARENTAL INDULGENCE
≠
STRONG CHARACTER

Adonijah's good looks and favored status mixed with a lack of parental leadership in his life turned out to be a nasty cocktail. This combination produced a wannabe king with no character to guide and sustain him.

HE CONSPIRED TO BE THE BOSS

Adonijah's sense of entitlement led him not only to *aspire*, but also *conspire*, to be the next king.

"He conspired with Joab son of Zeruiah and with Abiathar the priest. They supported Adonijah..." (1 Kings 1:7)

Since David wasn't going to appoint Adonijah to kingship, he attempted to promote himself. He got all of his cronies together and laid out a plan.

"...but Zadok the priest, Benaiah son of Jehoiada, Nathan the prophet, Shimei, Rei, and David's warriors did not side with Adonijah. Adonijah sacrificed sheep, oxen, and fattened cattle near the stone of Zoheleth, which is next to En-rogel. He invited all his royal brothers and all the men of Judah, the servants of the king, but he did not invite Nathan the prophet, Benaiah, the warriors, or his brother Solomon." (1 Kings 1:8-10)

If you find yourself scheming, prying, pushing, and subverting the powers that be to get your next job, relationship, or leadership position - please just stop! It has never worked for me throughout my entire life when I've tried to force my way into something. It is so much better to prepare and pray than to pry and push. Positions that find you tend to work out better than those you had to kick doors open for. There's so much wisdom in learning to flourish where you're planted, sprout where you are, and be content in your current tent.

Most of the time, if you aren't happy where you are, you won't be satisfied at the next place, either. You may think: "But it's harder where I'm at." Trust me, it's going to be challenging wherever you go!

I've pastored seven churches over thirty plus years. At every church, there are the same type of people and the same type of problems! They simply go by a different name. After you are at the new place long enough, you will think, "I remember that person. They must go by another name now."

The point is if you can't be happy where you are, you won't be happy where you are going. Don't pry or push. Allow the discontentment you feel to lead you in prayer and preparation.

I affectionately call my current pastoral role at Cross Church my *Yankee job*. For those not tuned into the sports world, that simply means that it's my dream job. I worked for thirty years to be able to serve in this capacity, at this place. Yet when I was called to be the pastor here, I intentionally played the slow game.

Before I started pastoring at Cross Church, I moved back home to Oklahoma to pastor a church there. Honestly, our family loved where we were at and didn't want to go back. We had planted a church in Arizona, but the economy was terrible during the recession of 2008, and I had to find a more stable job to support our family. Even though the church in Oklahoma was full of good and Godly people, it wasn't where our hearts truly wanted to be.

Can I say something unpopular to the current generation? Sometimes you just need to work, even if you don't like where you're working. I took the position in Oklahoma even though it wasn't my first choice. Where you want to be isn't always where you need to be! Honestly, the first year I was pretty depressed and subtly pouted the entire time. But I slowly got out of the funk, and I decided to make the most out of where I was. I convinced myself I'd be there forever, and therefore worked on learning to like it. And do you know what's wild? I *actually* did come to enjoy it. And even better, God did some special stuff while I was there.

I was intentional to immerse myself in the local culture. I even went as far as to buy some cows! In full transparency, that wasn't a far stretch for me as I grew up on a cattle farm. If I won the lottery tomorrow, my first purchase would probably be another cattle farm.

I was in line at a local feed store one day when my cell phone rang. It was a guy named Bruce Ford, who was the interim pastor at the church I'm at now. He said, "Hey, Jack - I just wanted to call and ask you, would it be okay if I gave your name to the search committee at my church?"

Truth be told, I had become so faithful to the church in Oklahoma that I felt like I needed to just stay planted. I told him no thanks, hung up the phone, and didn't talk to Bruce for over three months. Finally, around Christmas, we connected again, and I felt God leading me to investigate the opportunity a little further.

It's so much better when God brings an opportunity to you instead of you trying to force an opportunity. I decided in my heart that I shouldn't pry, force, or push my way into a new situation simply because my current assignment wasn't my preference. Can I encourage you? Bloom where you're planted. Be content in your current tent. Let the opportunity find you.

I meet all sorts of young pastors and leaders who have amazing hearts. One problem I see at times, though, is a lot of them want to have a larger voice at the table. And I understand it. In fact, I've been there. I also don't want you to misunderstand me. Some of the best voices at the table today are young pastors and leaders. But if you want a larger voice, learn to develop your voice where you are currently planted. Small stages aren't insignificant stages! When you steward little well, bigger will find you.

Try making your number one priority serving your current organization instead of elevating yourself to a better organization. If you do a great job, others will knock down the door, trying to figure out what God's doing in your life. People and positions will find you.

Adonijah didn't want to wait on a process. He aspired and then conspired. If he had studied Israel's history, he might have been more willing to wait. The Bible is full of guys that had to be patient.

Take Moses, for example. The man who would eventually free the Israelites from Egypt's rule was raised by the Egyptians. As a punishment for a murder that he committed there, he was exiled from his homeland. He ended up on the backside of the desert, married a good-looking lady, and had some kids. Moses' life was all you could ask for! But then, as he often does, God interrupted it all. He showed up and basically said, "Moses, I want you to be the leader of the known world. You're going to become the emancipator of my people. Go back to Egypt and tell Pharaoh to set my people free."

Moses responded with an emphatic, "Nah, I'm good, God. You can keep talking crazy all you want, but I'm going to stay here with my girl."

God wouldn't relent, and Moses went on to free God's people from slavery and become their leader. God did something unbelievable with Moses' life. But it was after years of nothingness and anonymity in the backside of the desert.

Joseph is another case study in waiting. God gave Joseph a dream to lead at an early age, but it took forever to play out. It also took some strange turns, as Joseph became a slave and then a prisoner. Neither of those circumstances typically lend to leadership opportunities.

For those of you who think, "man, my situation's tough," consider Joseph for a second!. He was cut off from his family and forced into a culture that worshiped pagan gods. He was apparently the only man who worshiped the one true God in all of Egypt. He had no support system whatsoever for his beliefs or values. There was nowhere to turn to for Godly advice. To make matters worse, his boss, Pharaoh, was considered a god by the Egyptians. Joseph's wife was an Egyptian woman, and his father-in-law a priest of the sun god.

And it was in that climate that Joseph had to wait on

God to promote him to lead. It seemed not only improbable but also impossible. But Joesph waited, was faithful even in prison, and God called him to something greater.

It's too bad Adonijah didn't take that approach. Instead, he tried to scheme his way into becoming the next king.

He ended up making what business leaders call a CLM - a career-limiting move. Have you ever seen someone in your organization make one? Let's dive a little bit further into what those look like.

CAREER LIMITING MOVES

King David responded by saying, "Call in Bathsheba for me." So she came into the king's presence and stood before him. The king swore an oath and said, "As the Lord lives, who has redeemed my life from every difficulty, just as I swore to you by the Lord God of Israel: Your son Solomon is to become king after me, and he is the one who is to sit on my throne in my place, that is exactly what I will do this very day." (1 Kings 1:28-30)

Adonijah and all the invited guests who were with him heard the noise as they finished eating. Joab heard the sound of the ram's horn and said, "Why is the town in such an uproar?" He was still speaking when Jonathan son of Abiathar the priest, suddenly arrived. Adonijah said, "Come in, for you are an excellent man, and you must be bringing good news."

"Unfortunately not," Jonathan answered him. "Our lord King David has made Solomon king." (1 Kings 1:41-43)

It was reported to Solomon: "Look, Adonijah fears King Solomon, and he has taken hold of the horns of the altar, saying, 'Let King Solomon first swear to me that he will not kill his servant with the sword.'"

Then Solomon said, "If he is a man of character, not a single hair of his will fall to the ground, but if evil is found in him, he dies." So King Solomon sent for him, and they took him down from the altar. He came and paid homage to King Solomon, and Solomon said to him, "Go to your home." (1 Kings 1:51-53)

Adonijah learned the hard way that you must be careful what you aspire and conspire for. There are repercussions to prying and pushing your way into a promotion. When you don't get it, your entire future in the organization may be in jeopardy.

Adonijah found out first hand how quickly and harshly those repercussions can come. He not only feared for his political future but for his own life as well.

Adonijah's future influence with the kingdom was significantly reduced because of his actions. Think about it. He could have been the number two in charge of a great empire. That's a pretty good job! But unfortunately, his presumptuous attitude got in the way. Because of that, he was terrified for his life.

Not only did Adonijah conspire and aspire, but he also eventually expired!

Something very interesting happens next in the story. In other words, the plot is about to clot! Do you remember Abishag, the 900 BC electric blanket? Some commentators think she might have been first-century Viagra! Wowzah!!

Adonijah let the dust settle for a while but couldn't help himself for too long. He asked Bathsheba if she would approach the king and get David's approval for the marriage of Adonijah and Abishag. Seems harmless on the surface, but there's more to the story.

The power structure was tricky in the Old Testament. By marrying David's mistress, the public would have assumed that David blessed Adonijah as the rightful heir to the throne. When Adonijah involved Bathsheba to pitch the marriage idea to David, what seemed innocent was actually an evil scheme. Solomon saw it for what it actually was and ordered Adonijah's death. His prideful sense of entitlement led to his execution.

Adonijah just couldn't get out of his own way. He continuously let his pride and ego completely ruin his personal contentment. Deep entitlement eventually led to his execution!

In the end, Adonijah not only committed a CLM but a CEM - a career-ending move!

If you're a boss and have people in your organization like Adonijah, you're not allowed to kill them! Even though you might want to, sometimes!! That's the difference between being a king and leading an organization. But I want to give you a good boss takeaway to help you navigate the Adonijah's in your life.

IT'S NEVER THE PERSON YOU FIRE THAT GIVES YOU TROUBLE, BUT THE PERSON YOU SHOULD HAVE FIRED AND DIDN'T.

I'm not advocating that you go back and fire everybody. But I am saying that you can't let a couple of bad apples spoil the whole bunch. Entitled people are contagious and slowly spread their cancer throughout the entire organization. The best thing you can do to treat cancer is to remove it. It's painful, but the health of your organization is worth it.

And finally, if you're an employee and work for someone you can't submit to, please do everybody a favor and leave. If you can't follow, you don't deserve leadership.

As this chapter comes to an end, let me reassure you:

Be supportive.
Wait your turn.
Don't pry and push.
Let the position find you.

When you finally step into the role you've been working for your entire life, you'll find the wait to be worth it. You'll be able to lead as yourself, not a presumptuous version of who you think you're supposed to be.

GOOD BOSS REFLECTION + APPLICATION

Have your career opportunities been doors that God opened for you or ones you've forced open yourself? If you are a person that forces doors open, ask God to reveal why you don't trust him fully with your future.

What are some adjectives that describe entitled leaders? Would anybody use those words to describe your leadership style?

If you're the leader of an organization, do you have a succession plan in place? Ask God to show you some people that can lead your organization past your lifespan.

FOUR

SOLOMON:
THE POWER-HUNGRY BOSS

> **"I CANNOT ACCEPT YOUR CANON THAT WE ARE TO JUDGE POPE AND KING UNLIKE OTHER MEN, WITH A FAVORABLE PRESUMPTION THAT THEY DID NO WRONG. IF THERE IS ANY PRESUMPTION IT IS THE OTHER WAY AGAINST HOLDERS OF POWER, INCREASING AS THE POWER INCREASES. "**

Lord Acton, Catholic historian, politician, and writer

I'm writing this book in 2020, one of the most peculiar years in history. For almost the entire year, the world has been battling the COVID-19 pandemic. In attempts to preserve health, we've spent much of the year in lock downs - controversial orders sanctioned by the government. Saying it's been a crazy year for all of us is an extreme understatement! As my pastor likes to say, "It was tougher than Walmart beef jerky."

There were so many things in our lives disrupted in 2020 - work schedules were changed, sporting events were canceled, and graduation ceremonies became drive-thru events. Our poor youngest daughter graduated from high school without the pomp and circumstance of the full-blown graduation ceremony she deserved. It was sort of a Debbie Downer.

Normally, when you go to graduation ceremonies, you hear speeches about life goals and ambitions. New graduates are inspired to bravely step into a new world with endless possibilities. Every graduation ceremony speech I've ever heard can be summed up with three exhortations: get an education, get a job, and then get rich. Those are the worldly ambitions of every high school graduate. Upon graduation, students aim to get an education to get a job to get rich. That way, they can buy a ritzy house, fancy cars, and retire wealthy.

In this chapter, we're going to learn how to be a better boss from the life and leadership of King Solomon. He was someone who lived by the goals and ambitions you hear about in graduation speeches. No one had an education, job, or riches, quite like Solomon. He was the wisest man to ever live, had the most important job of his day, and was the wealthiest man in history. He was the Bill Gates of his era.

However, Solomon was sort of an enigma in scripture. It's hard to pin down whether he was a good boss or a bad one from his character traits. In some ways, he represented the very best a boss could be; yet in other ways, the very worst.

When you look at Solomon's bad boss traits, you might be tempted to describe him as the *pleasure-hungry boss*. In his writings in the book of Ecclesiastes, he talks about his appetite for pleasurable things:

I said to myself, "Go ahead, I will test you with pleasure; enjoy what is good." But it turned out to be futile. I said about laughter, "It is madness," and about pleasure, "What does this accomplish?" I explored with my mind how to let my body enjoy

life with wine and how to grasp folly—my mind still
guiding me with wisdom—until I could see what is
good for people to do under heaven during the few
days of their lives. (Ecclesiastes 2:1-3)

We could also think about Solomon in terms of
the *money-hungry boss.* The book of 1 Kings describes him
in this way:

Solomon accumulated 1,400 chariots and 12,000
horsemen and stationed them in the chariot cities
and with the king in Jerusalem. The king made
silver as common in Jerusalem as stones, and he
made cedar as abundant as sycamore in the Judean
foothills. Solomon's horses were imported from
Egypt and Kue. The king's traders bought them from
Kue at the going price. A chariot was imported from
Egypt for 15 pounds of silver, and a horse for about
four pounds. In the same way, they exported them
to all the kings of the Hittites and to the kings of
Aram through their agents. (1 Kings 10:26-29)

But for the purposes of this chapter, let's think about
him in terms of the *power-hungry boss.*

Have you ever worked for a boss who cared more about
power than people? This can reveal itself in several ways.
Manipulation is often a favorite tool of the power-hungry
boss. These types of bosses also often mask their pursuit of
power behind the veil of being overly driven. But this leads
them to unhealthily drive people instead of leading them.
Pastors can be just as guilty of this as CEOs. Speaking from

experience, pastors should continually check their motives for wanting churches to grow and ministry platforms to expand.

Solomon's power allowed him to have wealth, enjoy pleasure, and, unfortunately, use people for his own personal gain. Solomon had an education and was even known by other world leaders as the wisest man throughout mankind. Upon taking the throne, God told Solomon that he would grant the king anything he wanted. Solomon surprisingly replied by requesting wisdom. God gave him that and then some. Yet, for a wise man, he made many foolish mistakes.

No one had a better job than Solomon. Solomon succeeded his father, David, as King of Israel. He ruled on that throne successfully for many years, accomplishing things that no previous king had. His prestigious job and education led to wealth we could never even imagine. In fact, Solomon was the wealthiest man in the world, which was a crucial component in making him the most powerful man in the world.

Solomon's story is of a boss who started out tremendously and yet ended tragically. And it's not because he failed professionally or financially. Even worse, he fell apart personally.

During Solomon's lifetime, we know that he wrote three books. The first was the Song of Solomon, which was a book of romance and passion. As a middle-aged man, he wrote the book of Proverbs, which was a book of practicality. Later in life, he wrote Ecclesiastes, - philosophical writing that questioned the deeper meaning of life. While there were undoubtedly slivers of hope in

Ecclesiastes, much of the book described the tension of emptiness and discontentment. Over and over, the wisest and wealthiest man in the world proposed that life was meaningless, meaningless, meaningless. The progression of Solomon's writings shows us a lot about his life. He started out filled with passion and ended full of pessimism. As you read Solomon's memoirs, you have to conclude that something went terribly wrong. The most powerful man in the world was left wondering if life had any purpose. John Action said, "Power tends to corrupt and absolute power corrupts absolutely."[1] Certainly, we see that in the life of Solomon, the power-hungry boss.

There is a word of caution here to bosses, especially really successful ones. The more successful and powerful you become as a leader, the more careful you need to be. Unguarded strengths can become massive weaknesses in our lives, as we see from Solomon.

So what lessons can we glean from his life that will prevent us from being destroyed by the very success we seek?

PUBLIC SUCCESS AND PRIVATE DRIFT

First of all, it's important to realize that you can lead well publicly and drift horribly privately. Think of a business leader, for example. Their profit margins can be great while their personal lives are a dumpster fire. In fact, the very things that contribute to professional success can also contribute to personal spirals. That's true in the secular and sacred world. If you're a pastor, it's possible for your church to be growing and your life to be failing.

Gordon McDonald, in his book, *Ordering Your Private Life*, says concerning his own life, "My success, my salary, my career, all moved upward. I was caught in a golden cage."[2]

What an interesting way to describe a successful life, yet one far from God's intentions. Solomon certainly was caught in a golden cage. Perhaps you live in a place right now, professionally, where everything is up and to the right. Your salary and profit margins are continuously growing while you're simultaneously getting every promotion imaginable. Maybe you're one of those pastors or leaders who turns everything into gold. You have the Midas touch. And yet, personally, you're struggling. You are caught in a golden cage. One that looks good externally but has you trapped internally.

We see the effects of the golden cage on Solomon's life:

So all the work Solomon did for the Lord's Temple was completed. Then Solomon brought the consecrated things of his father David—the silver, the gold, and all the utensils—and put them in the treasuries of God's Temple. (2 Chronicles 5:1)

Solomon built Israel's first Temple, which would house God's presence and be the primary place of worship for God's people. What a fantastic God-honoring accomplishment for the young king! However, let's take a look at how Solomon's life progressed:

When Solomon was old, his wives seduced him to follow other gods. He was not completely devoted to Yahweh his God, as his father David had been. Solomon followed Ashtoreth, the goddess of the Sidonians, and Milcom, the detestable idol of the Ammonites. Solomon did what was evil in the Lord's sight, and unlike his father David, he did not completely follow Yahweh. (1 Kings 11:4-6)

One does not go from 2 Chronicles 5 to 1 Kings 11 overnight. It takes years of drifting. Solomon's years of poor small decisions resulted in a horrible outcome over time. The same guy who built the Holy Temple where thousands worshiped God is the same guy who erected Asherole poles to worship idols. How can that be?

Solomon arrived at the place many powerful men and women do. He thought the rules no longer applied to him - that he was above it all. And so, we find in 1 Kings 11 that he married multiple wives. That's a far cry from his heart that we see in his first book, the Song of Songs. In it, he tells us that he courted and married one woman. There was a time that this man who had 700 wives only had eyes for one special lady. How do you go from one to 700?! Throughout his career, he began to think that the rules didn't apply to him.

Out of his 700 partners, some of them were foreign. And the Bible says that these foreign wives brought foreign gods into Solomon's court, life, and leadership. They began to turn his heart away from the one true God.

Solomon is a textbook case of a spiritual drifter. The healthy place where he started was not the same place he ended. When asked what God could give him at the beginning of his leadership, Solomon only requested wisdom. And yet, in the end, he seemed to live very foolishly. So, the question is, how do we avoid drifting?

Drifting has terrible effects on personal, professional, and spiritual lives. There is perhaps more danger in the drift than in the middle of the fiercest storm.

My wife and I owned a boat for a short season, even though we knew nothing about boating. We had no clue how to load it on the trailer or take it off. On one occasion, we left the plug out and nearly sunk the boat in the middle of a nearby lake. It's safe to say that boating was always quite an experience for us.

On one occasion, we went out into the middle of Lake Pleasant just in time for a monsoon to stir up. If you're not familiar with Arizona and monsoons, they can just whip up out of nowhere during the summer months. This particular one caught us unaware and unprepared, as gigantic waves tossed and turned our boat in every which disorienting direction. Talk about scary! I undoubtedly thought we were going to capsize. Just days later, we decided to sell the boat. They say the two best days in a boat owner's life are the day they buy the boat and the one they sell it. Thankfully we survived to sell the boat and tell the story!

It's one thing to be caught up in an obvious, ferocious storm. When that happens, you quickly go home and list it on Offer Up. But it's another thing to drift without recognizing it. You can think you have set the anchor firmly just to find yourself in a completely different place from where you aimed to go. You might take a nap, wake up, and be miles away from where you started. I think that's how moving away from God's purpose for our business, careers, and goals happens. We think that we have anchored ourselves but begin to drift without realizing it. And one day, we wake up, and we're far from where God told us to go.

Reasons for drifting are hard to nail down. There may be more than one force at work in our lives that cause us to drift from God and others.

It could be we have the wrong influencers in our lives. As the old saying goes, "If you're going to fly with the eagles, you can't run with the turkeys." That's why it's so important to surround yourself with the right people and coaches who can keep you on target. We'll talk more about that later.

I think sometimes we drift simply out of complacency in our lives. We get to a place where everything seems great, so we stop our forward movement. That is true both professionally and spiritually. As the saying goes, "If you think you're green, you will grow; if you think you're ripe, you will rot." In life, there is no standing still. We are either moving forward or going backward in life. When we put our lives in neutral, drifting becomes inevitable.

In Solomon's life and ours, there is a persistent tug from the world, which tries to get us drifting away from God. Think about it like a constant undercurrent that wants to pull your boat out to sea. Even though you can't see it, it's there and isn't going away. Therefore, we must be intentional in combating the undercurrent that continually wants to pull us away from God and his best plans.

What's the solution? How do we avoid drifting? Clearly, we have to set some secure anchors that will help us remain where we're supposed to be. Let's look at what those anchors are:

#1 - The Anchor of Accountability

First of all, we need to set an anchor of accountability. I can't express how important it is to make sure we have others in our lives to who we are accountable. The crazy thing about success is that it inevitably leads to isolation. The higher up the ladder you climb, the fewer people you encounter who understand you. Mark it down: the higher the air, the fewer the peers. Therefore, there will be fewer people who understand your position to actually hold you accountable. Nonetheless, the importance of accountability doesn't change.

Some time ago, I heard a story about two men riding in a sleigh during an unexpected blizzard. They were freezing and terrified that they wouldn't reach home safely. They came upon another traveler who had fallen in the snow who was close to death. One of the two men on the sleigh pleaded with the other to stop and help him, but the other refused. The concerned one decided to stay with the traveler to stay and support, even though the delay could lead to his own death. His companion left his friend and stranger behind in life-threatening conditions. Working feverishly, the one who stayed continuously massaged the unconscious man's body. After what seemed like hours of labor, the unconscious traveler responded and revived to full body function. The two men got up and walked in the snow together back to shelter. The vigorous work of the man saved both of them. On the way to safety, they came across a sleigh. The man who had refused to stay died helpless and alone.

The energy we spend on relationships is never wasted. The need for accountability is never lost. Doing life with others is not only safer, but it's also better. It could mean the difference between life and death. Furthermore, it could mean the difference between surviving and thriving.

Years ago, I remember talking about banks and thinking they were too big to fail. And yet, many of them have collapsed since then. The banking industry taught us you must caution yourself from believing the myth you're too big not to fail. And how true that is in our personal lives? We become too big not to fail when we are too big to be held accountable.

When Solomon's father David failed, someone immediately stepped into his world and held him accountable. Nathan, the prophet, was close enough to David to hold him responsible and quickly provide some intense course correction.

Later in Solomon's life, as he became extremely successful, there was no Nathan in his life - nobody to hold him accountable. And oh, how we all need a Nathan. Men and women who will hold us accountable are crucial to our personal lives.

In his book, *Character That Counts*, Rod Handley says, "No substitute exists for personal accountability with other godly people. Secret sins have much more power and usually last much longer than those we acknowledged to our Christian brothers and sisters."[3]

We have to look for someone to attach our anchor of accountability to!

#2 - The Anchor of Authority

The second anchor that we need to set is that of authority. Solomon may have been a brilliant guy and perhaps even smartest in the room. But unfortunately, he was not more intelligent than God and his Word. Solomon needed a higher power, a higher voice, and a higher authority. We have a motto in our church that says: you're entitled to your own opinion, but not your own Bible. That simply means that the Bible needs to trump everything else in our lives. Solomon would have benefited from obediently listening to authority that held the trump card to his own wisdom and success.

Years ago, my wife and I used to play the card game Spades with some other couples. In the game, spades are the trump cards. If you have a spade, you'll take the hand and win the game. A two-of-spades will trump even the king-of-diamonds.

Well, God's word is the trump card. The authority of the Bible trumps all personal opinions in our lives. God's word is to become the most powerful authority in our life. This is tested when we discover that God's word says one thing, but our lives suggest another. We can't try to adjust the Bible to fit our lives; we adjust our lives to fit the Bible. End of story!

We must anchor our lives to the authority of God's word.

PROJECTS OVER PEOPLE

Besides drifting, there's a second problem we discover in Solomon's life. He didn't use his position to serve people.

When you have power, you can use your position to build people or use people to build your position. Unfortunately, Solomon wasn't known as someone who put others before his ambitions. Simply put, he chose projects over people. After Solomon's death, Israel was wrangling over who would be their next king. As next up in line, the people had one request from Solomon's son, Rehoboam. They hoped he would care for the people he was to lead.

"Your father made our yoke harsh. Therefore, lighten your father's harsh service and the heavy yoke he put on us, and we will serve you." (2 Chronicles 10:4)

Isn't it interesting that people weren't impressed by Solomon's success, wisdom, or wealth? They didn't remember him by the temple he built or projects he completed. After his death, they recalled how harsh and heavy-handed he was. They remembered how he treated them poorly as fellow human beings. His legacy wasn't one they were looking for the next king to continue. They simply desired someone to lighten their load.

Everything that glitters is not gold. Just because the exterior of an organization looks impressive doesn't mean it is internally healthy. Too often, we are guilty of judging a book by its cover. Growing numerical metrics doesn't always indicate health. In Solomon's case, he had abused people to the point that they were actually happy when he died. Furthermore, they were hopeful that the next king would treat them better.

THE PURPOSE OF YOUR POSITION IS TO BUILD PEOPLE, NOT PROJECTS.

Regardless of what it is, the purpose of your position is to build people, not projects or products. Let me say that again: the purpose of your position is to build people, not projects or products. I've actually come to believe that the real purpose of leadership is building people. Period.

You may own a manufacturing company that builds widgets. But your primary job is not just to construct widgets with excellence. You have been placed there to build people. The people who work on the factory floor, in the offices, and the customers are the real reason you're there. People are more valuable than widgets.

You may be a pastor of a growing church, which is great! But a large platform and more numerical success than the other churches in town should never be the primary goal. Please don't get caught up doing whatever it takes to build your brand and platform your preaching. Every platform you have been given is to serve people, not your ego. Every pastor's real goal is not to build his church but to build the people within it.

I am not saying that church growth isn't important. I'm saying that you shouldn't destroy the people who work for you to get there.

If you're a coach, it's easy to assume you're being measured based upon your win-loss record. And unfortunately, sometimes that may be the case. But in the very end, it will not be your win-loss record that determines your success. You are there to develop people, not a program! The impact you make on your team's lives has a much longer-lasting impact than a winning season.

In *Ordering Your Private World*, Gordon McDonald writes about the difference between bosses driven to build their own success and those motivated to build people. He says this about the self-centered ones: "There is usually a trail of bodies in the wake of the driven person. Where once others praised him for his seemingly great leadership, there soon appears a steady increase in frustration and hostility as they see that the driven person cares very little about the health and growth of human beings."[4]

Wouldn't it be a terrible thing to look back at your career and realize that people quietly resented your leadership and character? That's what happens when you're more concerned about projects, products, and positions than caring for people.

Solomon built an impressive temple, but he failed to build people. In the end, the kingdom he led was divided after his death. It wasn't divided during his life only because God promised his father, David, to keep it intact. But it was Solomon's sin that caused the division of the kingdom. The next leaders, Rehoboam and Jeroboam, were a product of Solomon refusing to care for his team. Because he chased power, that's all they knew how to do. They ended up splitting Israel in two, and it never recovered to full strength. All because one power-hungry boss decided to build his kingdom but did not build the people who made it. Don't make that mistake. See people before anything else!

True leaders are people-builders. Here are some simple ways you can build the people you lead:

Encouragement. This is a powerful tool in building up those on your team. Don't ever underestimate the importance of an encouraging word to someone. Honestly, most people are getting just the opposite daily from others in their life. It is so empowering when someone speaks life into us. People who are often encouraged more fully understand their God-given identity. Therefore, they lead out of wholeness and completeness. A simple pat on the back can go a long way!

Honesty. Being completely honest with people on your team is key to building them up. That doesn't mean you are harsh and ruthless with them while giving correction. However, encouragement without honest assessment is phony, fake, and people will see right through it. When you speak the truth in love, people know that you care and genuinely want them to excel to the next level of personal and professional development.

Training. Good leaders are continually looking for ways to take people to the next level. They see the potential in their people and know that they need to provide opportunities to learn and grow to tap into it. If you're not doing this, don't be surprised that your team stagnates. The best leaders on your team will be learners. But the example of being a lifetime learner starts with you!

Time. Great leaders don't live above their people;

they live with them. Nothing says you care more than accessibility. When leaders get so successful that they place themselves in an ivory tower, their team becomes resentful. That's why I am convinced that good leaders wander. They wander in and out of offices and workspaces. They show up at little league games and dance recitals. By their actions, they let their people know that they care about them as people, not just their production.

Laughter. Positive work environments and teams know how to have fun. Life is too short not to enjoy the company of those you work with. Far too often, we as leaders take ourselves too seriously by not allowing for self-deprecating humor. Trust me, the ability to laugh at yourself and with others is a wonderful team builder. A team that laughs together stays together.

Celebration. Celebrating the success of others communicates that you are for them. As the saying goes, "A friend is someone who goes on loving you no matter how successful either of you become." People builders are cheerleaders. They cheer and celebrate others regularly.

If we make people the primary focus of our leadership, the other metrics of success are sure to follow. How can they not?

OBLIVIOUS TO THE OBVIOUS

A final thought on Solomon is that he was oblivious to the obvious. This is so true for power-hungry leaders. Solomon was the richest man in the world and had built some of the world's most remarkable buildings. In the end, he threw the biggest parties and enjoyed the most lavish of lifestyles. If Robin Leach were around when Solomon was alive, he would have featured Solomon on *The Lifestyles of the Rich and Famous*.

However, it seems that Solomon was completely oblivious to the obvious. Obviously, he had earned much of his wealth on the backs of those he ruled over. So much so that when he died, the people breathed a sigh of relief.

The wisest man in the world seemed utterly unconcerned with the fate of the people who allowed him to become the wealthiest man in the world.

GOOD BOSS TAKEAWAY:

WHAT YOU DON'T SEE IS MORE IMPORTANT THAN WHAT YOU DO SEE.

Think about how this plays out in your office. If you're the boss, people may not share their real feelings about the workplace with you. As a matter of fact, the boss is usually the last person that they go to. But if every time you enter the room, the conversation stops or changes, you might have a problem. A wise leader will pick up on the obvious, instead of ignoring it, and try to find out what is wrong before it's too late.

In counseling circles, they teach you to pick up on incongruences. An incongruence is when people say one thing and yet behave or act entirely differently. As a leader who truly wants to build people, not just projects and products, you must be artful in your people skills. You must watch and listen for the unseen and unstated. It sounds impossible, but it's usually more obvious than you think. If Solomon would have taken the time to hear what people *weren't* saying and see what they *weren't* showing, his legacy may have been far different.

Just because your bottom line is winning doesn't mean the morale of your team is. Just because your growth chart at church is up and to the right does not mean your team's morale is following suit. As a matter of fact, it could be exactly the opposite. Especially if those who work for you feel that you are using them for your own selfish gain.

I suggest you routinely do what I call *pulse checks* with key team members. Pulse checks can be done regularly, but especially if you pick up any bad body language or negative vibes. God gives leaders who truly care about people the gift of intuition to know when something isn't quite right. When you feel that in somebody, pull them aside and check on their soul. Ask them how they are doing. Be bold enough to ask them if you've done something to offend them. Make sure they know you care for them as a person, not just as an employee.

This is what it looks like to be a people-first leader instead of a typical power-hungry leader that we see so often in our world today. I don't want you to turn out like Solomon. It would be terrible to resign or retire and find out that people are breathing a sigh of relief. Put people above the bottom-line, and watch them, along with the bottom-line, grow exponentially.

GOOD BOSS REFLECTION + APPLICATION

Are you currently anchored to accountability and authority? If not, who is a leader in your life that you can ask to help prevent you from drifting?

Which of the following people-building skills do you need to get better at: encouragement, honesty, training, time, laughter, or celebration? Write down a plan to implement one specific technique to grow in that area.

Have you been picking up any negative vibes from anyone on your team? Schedule a *pulse check* with them immediately!

FIVE

REHOBOAM: THE INATTENTIVE BOSS

"MY DEARLY LOVED BROTHERS, UNDERSTAND THIS: EVERYONE MUST BE QUICK TO HEAR, SLOW TO SPEAK, AND SLOW TO ANGER."

James 1:19

One of the traps of leadership is that we think it's all about us and seldom slow down to listen to others. However, great leaders are great listeners. They hear what people are saying and not saying. They interpret body language and know how to spot an incongruence a mile away.

How do bad bosses and leaders do in this category? Well, let's just say they are not so great at listening. In this chapter, we will meet Rehoboam, an inattentive king who was a lousy listener.

Israel is once again going through a leadership transition. Solomon, the third king of Israel, has passed away, and the kingdom needs a new ruler once again. Rehoboam was next in line to be installed as king.

Solomon had been an impressive peacetime king who built an excellent infrastructure for the kingdom. He constructed the Temple and palaces, where people would worship and interact with God. But as Solomon became more successful, he became a compromised leader, which dramatically affected the kingdom.

As Solomon's reign came to an end, the kingdom was on the verge of unraveling. The next king would need to have some unique leadership skills and qualities to bring a fragmented nation back together.

That's how we're introduced to Rehoboam.

Then Rehoboam went to Shechem, for all Israel had gone to Shechem to make him king. When Jeroboam son of Nebat heard about it, for he was still in Egypt where he had fled from King Solomon's presence, Jeroboam stayed in Egypt. They summoned him, and Jeroboam and the whole assembly of Israel came and spoke to Rehoboam: "Your father made our yoke difficult. You, therefore, lighten your father's harsh service and the heavy yoke he put on us, and we will serve you." (1 Kings 12:1-4)

Soon, we will find that Rehoboam disregarded the people's request for an understanding king. Alexander Maclaren, in his commentary on this passage, says that the story of Rehoboam is a "miserable story of imbecility and arrogance."[1] It reveals that whatever leadership gifts Rehoboam may have possessed, he could not relate to people and understand their needs. Don't miss this: people skills are way more valuable than they might seem on the surface.

Later on, we will see Rehoboam received counsel from older men about what to do with the request, "lessen this yoke upon us." Afterward, he also got the counsel of some younger men. Unfortunately, he chose to take the advice of the wrong counsel. He listened to the overly ambitious younger men and made the yoke more intense. As a result, the kingdom became divided as the people rebelled against Rehoboam's leadership.

Rehoboam lacked the ability to relate to people and their needs.

Steve Saccone wrote a wonderful book called *Relational Intelligence*.[2] It explains why really smart leaders do really dumb things. Have you ever worked for somebody like that? Maybe you've had a boss who was brilliant but didn't understand his people whatsoever. In Relational Intelligence, Steve defines these types of people as relationally illiterate.

I think that's the story of Rehoboam - he suffered from low relational intelligence.

He reminds me of Michael Scott, the manager of the paper company, Dunder Mifflin, in the sitcom *The Office*. On one occasion, Michael was being interviewed for a job. He was asked about his strengths and weaknesses. He replied: "Well, my weaknesses are I work harder than I should, I care more than I ought to, and I invest too much time and effort in my work."

The interviewer looked at him a little bit puzzled and responded, "Well, what are your strengths?"

Michael said, "Don't you understand? My weaknesses and my strengths are the same things."

Michael had a complete lack of awareness of how he came off relationally. Some leaders are like that - they just don't get it. That's exactly how Rehoboam's story played out. We're going to see that he had very, very low relational intelligence. In other words, he was relationally challenged. And one of the biggest struggles for relationally challenged leaders is their ability to listen.

Rehoboam is the leader who wouldn't listen. Unfortunately, really bad listeners are usually really bad leaders. For this reason, we're going to call Rehoboam the *Inattentive Boss.*

HE WOULDN'T LISTEN TO HIS COUNSELORS

Then King Rehoboam consulted with the elders who had served his father Solomon when he was alive, asking, "How do you advise me to respond to these people?"

They replied, "Today if you will be a servant to these people and serve them, and if you respond to them by speaking kind words to them, they will be your servants forever."

But he rejected the advice of the elders who had advised him and consulted with the young men who had grown up with him and served him. (1 Kings 12:6-8)

The wise-counselors gave Rehoboam some really sound advice. They basically said, "Listen, what you need to do is work very hard in the early days of your leadership, endearing yourself to those whom you are called to lead. In return, they will endear themselves to you forever."

It would have required humility, time, and patience from Rehoboam. But I want you to write this down: great leaders know the value of humility, time, and patience. Meanwhile, not-so-great leaders run roughshod over the people God has called them to lead. The counselors knew this, and their wisdom warned to prevent it. Basically, the advice of the counselors was for Rehoboam to spend the early days of his leadership becoming likable.

Here's a simple yet powerful newsflash: when people like you, they're more likely to follow you!

Years ago, I read a little book by Tim Sanders called *The Likability Factor*.[3] The book's thesis was that people are much more willing to help you through life when you become likable. And right after I read that book, I had the opportunity to apply that principle to my life.

I was in San Diego with some other pastors from Arizona doing church assessments for the North American Mission Board. The last night we were there, we went down to the beach, ate dinner, and then walked along the shore. When I got back to the hotel room, I couldn't find my wallet anywhere. I'm not sure how you lose your wallet on a late-night beach walk with three preachers, but I did exactly that. To make things worse, it was a post 9/11 world, and I had to get on a plane the next morning. Security was extra tight, and having no identification just simply wouldn't fly! I had no idea how I was going to be allowed to get on a plane. With nothing to lose, I decided it was the time to implement lessons from *The Likability Factor*.

So, the next morning I went to the airport and walked up to the front desk. Confidently, I said, "Listen, I've got a problem. But I'm sure it's a problem you can handle because you look like the smartest person in the whole world! I'm sure you've seen this before and know what to do. Other people, maybe not so much - but I know you can help! I've lost my wallet, which means I have no form of identification. But I really need to get on that plane leaving for Phoenix in a few hours."

The lady was unbelievably kind to me. She helped me through a process, and after going through every conceivable search you could imagine, I got on the plane! I learned an invaluable lesson that day. When you're nice to people, they're more likely to like you. And when people like you, they're more likely to help you.

That's a key leadership thought and good boss takeaway.

GOOD BOSS TAKEAWAY:

PEOPLE ARE MORE INCLINED TO HELP YOU IF THEY LIKE YOU.

My encouragement to you is to write that down and live it out. Your leadership will go much smoother if the people you are leading actually like you. That was basically the elders' counsel to Rehoboam: win them over and spend time building positive relations. But instead of accepting that advice, he sought the advice of another group.

But he rejected the advice of the elders who had advised him and consulted with the young men who had grown up with him and served him. He asked them, "What message do you advise that we send back to these people who said to me, 'Lighten the yoke your father put on us'?"

Then the young men who had grown up with him told him, "This is what you should say to these people who said to you, 'Your father made our yoke heavy, but you, make it lighter on us!' This is what you should tell them: 'My little finger is thicker than my father's loins! Although my father burdened you with a heavy yoke, I will add to your yoke; my father disciplined you with whips, but I will discipline you with barbed whips.'" (1 Kings 12:8-11)

Now that is some bad advice! If you've just been hired to lead Dunder Mifflin, and the first day on the job, you make it twice as hard on your employees as the previous guy - it will not go well for you. If the last guy gave your staff raises and you instantaneously took them away, people would start looking for other employment. If the last guy gave employees bonuses and you stripped it from them to save more, you'd become the villain. If you made them work 60 hours a week instead of 40, they'd resent you for it. It's safe to say you would not be viewed as a benevolent or likable leader. It's also safe to say Rehoboam was not considered benevolent or likable by his people.

He ignored the advice of the right people, and took the advice of the wrong ones. He went shopping for wisdom that fit his predetermined narrative. In other words, he wanted advice that told him what he wanted to hear! Have you ever noticed how often people ask for advice, but don't really want it? He asked his wise counselors for advice and didn't like their answer, even though it was laced with wisdom. Many times we go searching for counsel with our minds already made up. We're simply shopping around for someone to tell us what we want to hear.

I've seen this play out in counseling environments over and over and over again. As a pastor, people will often come to me looking for advice. I always tell them what the Bible says, which sometimes results in them looking for a new counselor or even a new church! Why? All because the advice wasn't what they wanted to hear.

That's exactly what Rehoboam did. He received some great counsel and said, "Ah, that's not really the answer I was looking for. I'm going to find somebody who will validate what I want." So, he didn't listen to his counselors.

HE WOULDN'T LISTEN TO THE PEOPLE

He didn't listen to his counselors, and he didn't listen to the people either.

Jeroboam and all the people came to Rehoboam on the third day, as the king had ordered: "Return to me on the third day." Then the king answered the people harshly. He rejected the advice the elders had given him and spoke to them according to the young men's advice: "My father made your yoke heavy, but I will add to your yoke; my father disciplined you with whips, but I will discipline you with barbed whips."

The king did not listen to the people, because this turn of events came from the Lord to carry out His word, which the Lord had spoken through Ahijah the Shilonite to Jeroboam son of Nebat. When all Israel saw that the king had not listened to them, the people answered him:

"What portion do we have in David?
We have no inheritance in the son of Jesse.
Israel, return to your tents;
David, now look after your own house!" (1 Kings 12:12-16)

When a leader fails to listen, he will eventually fail to lead. In Rehoboam's story, the people of Israel rebelled against the king. They killed his messengers and divided the kingdom. Jeroboam became the king of the ten tribes of Israel. Rehoboam was left leading only the tribe of Judah, which contained the capital, Jerusalem.

When all Israel heard that Jeroboam had come back, they summoned him to the assembly and made him king over all Israel. No one followed the house of David except the tribe of Judah alone. (1 Kings 12:20)

The best churches, leaders, organizations, and companies are always asking this question: "How can we add value to the lives of those that we lead?"

GOOD BOSS TAKEAWAY:

IF YOU WANT TO HAVE A VOICE IN SOMEONE'S LIFE, YOU HAVE TO ADD VALUE TO THEIR LIFE.

The voices who carry the most influence have added the most value. That's why the best-of-the-best are always searching for ways to add value to the people they serve.

The company, Zappos, is a wonderful example of this. If you don't know about them, they are an online shoe store with a reputation for having a killer customer service department.

Zappos was created by a 24-year-old entrepreneur who sold a previous business to invest in the new one. Over time, he built his company to have 1,600 employees and over a billion dollars in sales each year. Zappos was founded to create the best customer service experience on the planet. They're not just in the shoe business but also the people business. If you call their customer loyalty hotline, you won't be sent to a tree of different voicemails or people who don't speak the same language as you. You will talk to a real person who is ready to help you, specifically.

Some time ago, after spending two days trying to talk to someone at the IRS, I decided to see how different the customer service experience would be at Zappos.

I had heard raving reviews about them. Furthermore, they did something within their customer service department that really intrigued me. Suppose you are a new employee going through orientation with Zappos and don't like it after two weeks. In that case, they pay you $2,000 just to go away.

So, I just called them up to see how friendly and likable they would be. Keep in mind that I've never bought any shoes from them. But I cold-called them, and before I even talked to a person, my experience was already off to a great start. When you call Zappos, a prerecorded message says,

"Hey, thanks for calling! We're going to get your assistant right away, but if you'd like to hear the joke of the day, press five."

Who wouldn't want to hear the joke of the day? By the way, the joke of the day was: "Why was the Thanksgiving soup so expensive? Because it had 24 carrots in it." (LOL)

So after a good laugh, a friendly young lady came on the phone and asked how she could help me. I told her that I'd never bought any shoes from Zappos and wasn't a customer, just an admirer. I also let her know that I was a preacher in need of an illustration for my upcoming message on Sunday. First, I asked her if they really gave disgruntled trainees $2,000 to walk away. Next, I asked if she has enjoyed her time at Zappos.

She responded, "Yeah, it's true! If you don't like our company's culture, they'd rather you leave than to stay. I love it here! It's the first place I've ever worked where the leaders really care about their employees."

Wow! Did you hear what the Zappos evangelist said? Zappos leaders really care about their employees!

People like her will excel at caring for customers. Why? Because her bosses care about her. As a matter of fact, the CEO at Zappos does not have a corner office. His desk is in the middle of the cubicles where everybody else works, amongst those he cares about.

Remember, accessibility is an enormous sign that you are a listening leader. Maybe you've heard the concept that *leaders leak*. That means vision leaks out of them while they're around those they lead. I've also found it true that *leaders wander*. They wander in and out of the offices of those they lead, always around their people. The best policy a leader could have is an open-door policy. It is impossible to be a great leader and listener if you're not open to those you lead.

Zappos got it right, while Rehoboam got it terribly wrong. If you want to have a voice in someone's life, you must add value to them.

HE WOULDN'T LISTEN TO GOD

Finally, Rehoboam didn't listen to God. In fact, his most glaring weakness was that he didn't listen to the very God he served.

Now Rehoboam, Solomon's son, reigned in Judah. Rehoboam was 41 years old when he became king; he reigned 17 years in Jerusalem, the city where Yahweh had chosen from all the tribes of Israel to put His name. Rehoboam's mother's name was Naamah the Ammonite.

Judah did what was evil in the Lord's eyes. They provoked Him to jealous anger more than all that their ancestors had done with the sins they committed. They also built for themselves high places, sacred pillars, and Asherah poles on every high hill and under every green tree; there were even male cult prostitutes in the land. They imitated all the detestable practices of the nations the Lord had dispossessed before the Israelites. (1 Kings 14:21-24)

How often do we get caught up in our own pursuits

and agendas, just to forget that the main thing in our lives is to hear and obey the voice of our God? The Bible says over and over again that we need to listen to him.

At the Mount of Transfiguration, God spoke and told Jesus' disciples: "This is my Son, the chosen one; listen to Him!" (Luke 9:35)

In his prophecy in Revelation, God told the church: "Anyone who has an ear should listen to what the Spirit says..." (Revelation 2:7)

Does God still speak to us today? Absolutely!

In 2018, Tony Dungy was commentating on the upcoming Super Bowl. He stated that Nick Foles, the quarterback of the Philadelphia Eagles, had a great chance of leading his team to the Super Bowl. His reasoning was that Nick had been listening to the Lord and had a spirit of confidence and peace.

As you can imagine, he took some grief from the secular world for that comment. However, on Twitter, Dungy responded to his critics, "Why would you find it hard to believe that the Holy Spirit could speak to Nick Foles just as much as a coach could speak to him? If he credited a coach for saying, 'Stay calm and be confident,' that's good. But if he tells me Christ says that to him, I shouldn't report it?"[4]

For the leader tuned into the voice of God, the Holy Spirit can speak into your life. God speaks to us through his word, wise counsel, and his Holy Spirit.

How much different would your life, business, family,

and organization be if you, as the leader, regularly tuned in to the voice of God?

Great leaders listen to wise counsel and the people around them. They understand how to read the tea leaves in the office. They interpret both the verbal and nonverbal communication around them. Most importantly, great leaders listen to God and obey his voice. They take the advice of the Father, who says, "This is my Son; the chosen one; listen to Him."

GOOD BOSS REFLECTION + APPLICATION

Would those who you lead consider you likable? Put yourself in their shoes and think about what it would be like to work for yourself.

Are you more likely to take good advice or the advice you want to hear? When is the last time you followed the advice of wise counsel even though their wisdom was hard to hear?

Do you slow down to ask God about the big decisions you have to make? Try asking him before you ask everybody else.

SLY

JEROBOAM:
THE INSECURE BOSS 2.0

"I'VE GOT SCARS ON MY SOUL THAT I'M SCARED TO SHOW. I CRIED IN THE MORNING BUT YOU'D NEVER KNOW. I SHOULD LET IT BE, IT'S JUST MY INSECURITIES."

Jess Glynne, Singer & Songwriter

If you remember chapter one - and I hope you do - we gave Saul the nickname of the *insecure* boss. Leadership insecurity is so important to address that I want to circle back around to it a second time.

We often see leaders who are not comfortable in their own skin, can't celebrate when others succeed, and fear losing power more than anything else. Those qualities are a sure recipe for failure.

Thankfully, I learned about the issue of insecurity at an early age. At my first full-time pastorate, I was quickly faced with the task of becoming comfortable with my identity in Christ. The source of my self-worth was a significant challenge in that season. I was 27 years old and had all the insecurities that come with being a lead pastor at a young age.

On top of that, I had some big shoes to fill! The church I was pastoring had only had three pastors in its 40-year history. And the 27-year-old me was the third. But wait, it gets better. All three of us were members of the church at the same time! The founding pastor and the beloved previous pastor were still heavily involved. In fact, the pastor who served before me was a childhood hero of many people in town and led the church to tremendous success. He stayed on staff as an evangelist.

I was the first pastor in the church's history who didn't start it or grow up there. Both of the previous pastors were justifiably loved by the church. They had a voice of authority there that I would never grow into. But despite many awkward moments over my 7-year tenure, I learned a valuable lesson that has served me well: God's people are capable of loving more than one person or pastor at a time.

If you're a boss, leader, coach, or pastor and you always feel threatened by your predecessors or possible successors, then let me give you some advice. Stop it! It's okay for your staff to love and respect others that have come before you. As a matter of fact, that should give you some hope that one day they will come to love and respect you if they don't already.

In his book, *Good Boss, Bad Boss*, Robert Sutton lists several qualities of a good boss:

- "A good boss has strong opinions and weakly held beliefs."
- "A good boss does not treat others as if they are idiots."
- "A good boss asks a lot of questions."
- "A good boss does not hesitate to say, 'I don't know.'"
- "A good boss forgives people when they fail, remembers the lessons, and teaches them to everyone."
- "A good boss fights as if he is right and listens as if he is wrong."
- "A good boss expresses gratitude to his people or her people."[1]

I hear Sutton saying that a good boss is secure in who

they are. Internal security allows them to lead in a healthy, positive manner. They celebrate others and look for ways to platform their success.

However, insecure leaders don't do that as they can't bring themselves to. Because they're fearful of people and uncomfortable in their own skin, they never raise up others to lead.

THE IDOLATRY OF INSECURITY

Insecurity marks the story of Jeroboam. When you read his story in 1 Kings, you find that he had a tremendous fear of losing power. Bad bosses fear losing power more than they fear losing life itself. I want you to see how insecurity played out in Jeroboam's story.

Remember our buddy, Solomon? He was the extremely educated, successful, and rich king who took the throne after his father, David. In case you need a friendly reminder, Solomon's leadership was marked with high-highs and low-lows. He built the temple where all of Israel would come to worship God, but also married evil women who led him to serve other gods. Because Solomon couldn't stay on the strait and narrow, he created some repercussions for his family.

Rehoboam, his son, took over Israel's kingship after his dad's death. But because of Solomon's sin, God had previously promised to tear a portion of the kingdom away from Solomon's family and give it to one of his servants. Before Rehoboam even took the throne, he was destined to fail.

This is where Jeroboam entered the story in a significant

way. He had been a high-ranking official in Solomon's administration. Because of how industrious he was, he was put in charge of Solomon's entire labor force. He served Solomon faithfully. But upon the king's death, God chose Jeroboam to initiate the punishment for Solomon's sin. As Rehoboam started making stupid decisions, most of the nation revolted against him and requested to be led by Jeroboam instead.

We see God's plan to punish Solomon, strip a majority of the kingdom from Rehoboam, and appoint Jeroboam to kingship, play out below:

"However, I will not take the whole kingdom from his hand but will let him be ruler all the days of his life because of My servant David, whom I chose and who kept My commands and My statutes. I will take 10 tribes of the kingdom from his son's hand and give them to you. I will give one tribe to his son, so that My servant David will always have a lamp before Me in Jerusalem, the city I chose for Myself to put My name there. I will appoint you, and you will reign as king over all you want, and you will be king over Israel." (1 Kings 11:34-37)

When all Israel heard that Jeroboam had come back, they summoned him to the assembly and made him king over all Israel. No one followed the house of David except the tribe of Judah alone. (1 Kings 12:20)

Welcome to the divided kingdom! Israel became two

territories with two kings. Rehoboam, Solomon's son and successor, became king of Judah, which held the holy city of Jerusalem and the Temple. And Jeroboam became King of Israel - the leader of ten other tribes of God's people. The Boam' Boys were pinned against each other!

Jeroboam had a larger kingdom; however, Rehoboam ruled over the sacred place of worship. To worship God, all of Jeroboam's people had to travel to Rehoboam's kingdom. This proved problematic, considering Jeroboam had stripped a large chunk of Rehoboam's kingdom from him. Talk about relational tension.

The last thing Jeroboam wanted was the people of his kingdom going to Rehoboam's kingdom to worship at the Temple. As the newly appointed leader, Jeroboam feared that his people may desire to return to their old leader if they got spiritually attached to his land. Because of his personal issues, Jeroboam had insecure worries: *What will happen if my people keep going to Judah to worship? What if they develop an allegiance to Rehoboam and want to unify the kingdom again?! I'll lose all of my power!*

So Jeroboam hashed out a plan. He set up an altar at Dan, and another at Bethel, so the people could stay home to worship God rather than travel to Rehoboam's land.

Then he made two golden calves, and he said to the people, "Going to Jerusalem is too difficult for you. Israel, here is your God who brought you out of the land of Egypt." He set up one in Bethel, and put the other in Dan. This led to sin; the people walked in procession before one of the calves all the way to Dan. (1 Kings 12:28-29)

Under the guise of making it easier for them to worship, he exposed an entire nation to idolatry. And it was all an attempt to cover up his own insecurities.

The church I lead, Cross Church, has an international campus in Myanmar. Over the years, I have visited this amazing country numerous times, and we have sent multiple teams to work there. Myanmar had a democratic leader who won a congressional gold medal. In his acceptance speech, he quoted Aung San Suu Kyi by saying, "It is not power that corrupts but fear."[2]

Fear of losing power corrupts those who wield it. That's exactly what we see play out in the life of Jeroboam, the insecure king. The fear of losing your power will corrupt you as a leader. Fear in the lives of leaders is an issue of idolatry. It happens when you place position, power, or prominence on the throne and value it above all else. It caused Jeroboam to rewrite history, and not in the right way! He basically said, "Hey, those golden calves - they're a reminder of God's deliverance."

It wasn't the first time Israel had worshiped a golden calf. Right after being freed from slavery in Egypt, while wandering around the wilderness, they built a golden calf and worshipped it at Mount Sinai. Jeroboam referenced this when he tried to convince the people that a golden calf represented God's deliverance. His manipulative reasoning simply wasn't valid.

Israelites who worshiped the golden calf in the wilderness never got to enter God's promised land. Jeroboam knew that the calves weren't of God, yet led his people to worship them anyway. In doing so, he practically became an atheist - using religion to satisfy his own selfish desires and goals.

As leaders, we have to exercise great restraint when it comes to the golden calves that we make objects of worship. Success, profit reports, and church attendance can all become golden calves.

SERVING PEOPLE VS. PLEASING PEOPLE

As Simon Sinek says in his book, Together is Better, "Leadership is not about being in charge. Leadership is about taking care of those in your charge."[3]

By the end of this book, we will see selfless leadership masterfully played out by the best boss to ever do it – Jesus Christ. But for now, just know that healthy leadership is a calling to improve the lives of those we lead.

GOOD BOSS TAKEAWAY:

HEALTHY LEADERSHIP IS A CALLING TO IMPROVE THE LIVES OF THOSE WE LEAD.

It makes no difference what type of organization you're in charge of. You're simply there to improve the lives of those you lead. You are not there to gain notoriety, increase your income, or get to the next level.

All of those things may indeed come your way as a leader, but they are not the reason God has placed you in your current position of leadership. In chapter five, we talked about how adding value to others gives you a voice in their lives. We get this principle upside down when we think the organization is there to serve us, instead of the other way around. Even worse, when it becomes about us, the accolades we covet become idols in our lives. Success, salary, notoriety, and influence become the calves we worship. We're even willing to sacrifice the well-being of others to obtain them.

Think about this. The most remarkable example of leadership throughout history is Jesus. Yet, it was never about him. Time and time again, he exemplified how to be selfless instead of selfish. He washed his disciples' feet, fed the hungry, and healed the sick. In essence, the ultimate leader was the ultimate servant.

"...just as the Son of Man did not come to be served, but to serve, and to give His life - a ransom for many." (Matthew 20:28)

How different Jeroboam was from Jesus. To guard his popularity and keep people away from his perceived competition, he led his people to shift their worship from God-centered to man-centered. Eventually, it brought down the entire nation.

Along the way, Jeroboam forgot something fundamental: *his position was a gracious gift.* I think sometimes leaders, unfortunately, forget that as well. Whether you lead an organization, church team, community group, or your family - don't forget that your calling is a gracious gift from God. Gifts from God are to be stewarded for whatever time he allows you to have them. Instead, Jeroboam saw this gift as something to be clinched tightly. He looked at leadership as something to be protected rather than stewarded.

I once had a conversation with a lady who was a high-level leader in a massive company in Arizona. Although the company appeared to be successful, they were weeding people out and letting them go like crazy. She had every reason to fear for her job. But I loved her perspective. She said, "Pastor, I've come to a realization: if God wants me here, he will keep me here. I don't have to try to finagle my way into things. I don't have to become something I'm not. If God doesn't want me here anymore, he will surely move me elsewhere."

That's a person who is more fearful of God than people! She was a God-pleaser, not a people-pleaser. Leaders who trust God with their future aren't afraid of losing their power or position.

Have you ever been in a position like that? Maybe you're in a situation like that right now. Who do you trust in the moments when your job security or success of your company is shaky, to say the least? Jeroboam should have trusted in the God who approved of him, but instead, he twisted things to keep his people's approval. His people, not God, became the controlling factor. Bad bosses fear people and try to please them more than God.

If you follow politics, you know that there's so much polarization within our country's leadership. I pray that one day God will raise up a leader who doesn't care which side of the aisle you're on. We need politicians who don't make decisions based on the polls or how the wind of popular opinion is blowing. It would be refreshing if God raised up congressmen, congresswomen, presidents, and governors who said, "I know that I've been elected by the people. But my best gift to the people is to fear God. I'm going to vote and lead accordingly."

Fearless voices could change the pulpits of our country. Preaching would be much more effective if preachers would stand up and stop trying to tickle people's ears. The truth is, the Bible isn't always comfortable for everyone but is still useful. People can only live according to the Bible when preachers choose to please God over people.

Jeroboam's big mistake was that he got everything out of order. He thought his number one job was to keep the people happy. But his job, as God's appointed king, was much more significant than that. He was to follow God and lead others to follow him as well.

THE APPROVAL OF ONE

When leaders prioritize power and people-pleasing, there will always be a price to pay.

A man of God came from Judah to Bethel by a revelation from the Lord while Jeroboam was standing beside the altar to burn incense. The man of God cried out against the altar by a revelation from the Lord: "Altar, altar, this is what the Lord says, 'A son will be born to the house of David, named Josiah, and he will sacrifice on you the priests of the high places who are burning incense on you. Human bones will be burned on you.'" He gave a sign that day. He said, "This is the sign that the Lord has spoken: 'The altar will now be ripped apart, and the ashes that are on it will be poured out.'" (1 Kings 13:1-3)

Fast forward 200 years:

When the Lord tore Israel from the house of David, Israel made Jeroboam son of Nebat king. Then Jeroboam led Israel away from following the Lord and caused them to commit great sin. The Israelites persisted in all the sins that Jeroboam committed and did not turn away from them. Finally, the Lord removed Israel from His presence just as He had declared through all His servants the prophets. So Israel has been exiled to Assyria from their homeland until today. (2 Kings 17:21-23)

What a legacy! After so much promise, 200-years later, Jeroboam was the one blamed for an entire nation's destruction. And as predicted, a new king emerged who's name was Josiah. How different Josiah was from Jeroboam. He was eight years old when he started ruling and became one of the greatest kings Israel ever knew.

I once heard somebody say, "The best way to identify a crooked stick is to lay a straight stick next to it." Let's lay this straight stick, Josiah, next to that crooked stick, Jeroboam.

What do we know about Josiah?

Josiah was eight years old when he became king and reigned 31 years in Jerusalem. He did what was right in the Lord's sight and walked in the ways of his ancestor David; he did not turn aside to the right or the left. (2 Chronicles 34:1-2)

When you lay these two sticks next to each other, you see that Josiah loved the people and feared God. Jeroboam loved his power, only cared about people opinions in order to protect his position, and didn't fear God.

GOOD BOSS TAKEAWAY:

THE BEST LEADERS LOVE THEIR PEOPLE AND FEAR GOD.

Ultimately, leadership is all about living our lives for the approval of one. When we make pleasing God our number one priority, we will love and lead people as he does. This completely eliminates the need for insecurity in our lives. When we see our leadership position as a gracious gift that God had given us to steward, and not something to be held with a clenched fist, it frees us to love and lead!

GOOD BOSS REFLECTION + APPLICATION

Do you compare yourself to those who have led before you or who might come after you? Ask God for confidence in who he created you to be.

Do you worship your position or power more than you do God? Analyze if you spend more time thinking about your job or your relationship with Jesus.

Are you always worried about what people might think of your decisions? Ask God to free you from the fear of man.

SEVEN

AHAB:
THE POWER-HUNGRY BOSS
2.0

"POWER TENDS TO CORRUPT AND ABSOLUTE POWER CORRUPTS ABSOLUTELY."

Lord Acton, Catholic historian, politician, and writer

I want you to imagine the worst boss you've ever had. Picture that two-legged devil that you worked for or maybe are even employed by now. What made them such a bad boss?

A bad boss is indeed a terrible thing. You've probably heard the saying, "People do not leave bad companies, but they leave bad bosses." I've found that to absolutely be true!

And with that being said, I want to introduce you to quite possibly the worst boss ever. This guy makes the worst boss you've ever had look like Mother Teresa. His name is Ahab, and he is flanked by an equally evil wife named Jezebel. There's a reason why nobody assigns the name Jezebel to their daughters!

RG Lee was the long-time pastor of Bellevue Baptist Church in Memphis, Tennessee. Many years ago, he preached a famous sermon called *Payday Someday*. It was a message based on Ahab and Jezebel's life. In the introduction to that sermon, he famously referred to Ahab as a "vile human toad that squatted on the throne of Israel" and Jezebel as a "poisonous snake that coiled alongside him."

What a way to introduce someone! Maybe your boss is like that - a vile human toad who squats at your workplace. Or possibly they're like a poisonous snake who is frequently coiled and ready to strike.

Here is the Old Testament commentary on the leadership ability of Ahab. Consider this the official employment review on Ahab's kingship.

"...Ahab did more to provoke the Lord God of Israel than all the kings of Israel who were before him."
(1 Kings 16:33)

Yikes! Of all the bad kings in the history of Israel, the Bible says that Ahab was the worst. Congrats, Ahab, you are the weakest link!

To say that he was the worst king Israel ever had is like saying that my dearly beloved Phoenix Suns basketball team is one of the worst ever. As I write this, they're having an exceptionally terrible year! If they really are the worst team ever, that's quite an accomplishment! There have been some awful NBA teams before them.

The same is true of Ahab. Between Saul's kingship and the Babylonians carrying Israel into captivity, there were 43 kings. Only a handful of them were actually godly, good leaders. So, to say that Ahab was the worst out of those 43 was quite an indictment. He was the "best worst boss ever." Maybe you've given a coffee mug like that to one of your bosses in the past.

To be the absolute worst boss of all time, what do you need to do? Let's examine the life of Ahab for answers.

THE BEST WORST BOSS EVER

To be the best worst boss ever, here's the first thing you need to do:

#1 - Cut Corners in Your Personal Life

But Ahab son of Omri did what was evil in the Lord's sight more than all who were before him. (1 Kings 16:30)

Terrible leaders regularly cut corners in their personal life. Just remember that who you are at home and in private will eventually come to roost for you in public. You can only compartmentalize for so long until your private and public lives cross-pollinate. Bad personal choices will eventually take root, grow, and become a public matter.

Bad bosses think they can cut corners in their personal life while being a stellar leader in public. This may indeed work for a short time, but if you want to lead well for a long time, you must pay attention to your private life. It's a good boss takeaway.

GOOD BOSS TAKEAWAY:

LEADERS LIVE AND LEAD OUT OF THE LEAK.

What do I mean by *the leak*? What is on the inside will eventually come out - it will naturally *leak* with no intentionality on your end whatsoever. That's a great thing if you're healthy inside. However, it's terrible news if there's some bad choices welt up inside of you. However, it is true, nonetheless, whether good or evil exists in you. We live, and we lead, out of the overflow of what is inside. So, when you look at Ahab, his kingdom's entire negative trajectory started with poor choices in his personal life. Don't miss that: everything wrong with Israel under his rule started with everything wrong inside him!

Without getting too far down into the weeds of Old Testament expectations for marriage, let's just say one of Ahab's biggest personal mistakes was that he married the wrong person. You can't get any more wrong than Jezebel. Suppose your son goes off to college and comes home after the first semester to introduce you to his new fiancée and says her name is Jezebel. I suggest you lock the doors and cast out the demons!

But the issue goes even further than marriage. As a leader, your personal life will be known and influenced by the company you keep. Ahab compromised in the most influential relationship of his life. He compromised in many other areas as well. What he thought were personal choices had far-ranging public implications. He cut corners in his personal life that cost him big time. When we compromise and cut corners, we create cracks in our character that will cost us later. Here's what I'm trying to say: CHARACTER MATTERS! When we compromise our character, we create cracks that will eventually be exposed.

Some time ago, Hurricane Maria hit the coast of Puerto Rico and caused substantial destruction. One of the most important things damaged was a dam that held water above a city of 70,000 people. The storm created a crack, and as a result, officials were concerned that the city needed to be evacuated. So, they sent out a message across the emergency management agency lines that said, "It could be tonight. It could be tomorrow. It could be in the next few days, but very likely, it will be soon."

The same is true of your character. Cracks that are small or even invisible to the naked eye can affect large amounts of people. Matters that you thought were personal have public implications, damaging your organization, business, church, or family. It may not be tonight, tomorrow, or even in a few days, but eventually, you'll be exposed.

Cutting corners in your personal life will corrupt your leadership ability. But if you aspire to be the worst boss ever, there's also a second thing you need to do:

#2 - Sacrifice Family on the Altar of Work

Ahab also made an Asherah pole. Ahab did more to provoke the Lord God of Israel than all the kings of Israel who were before him.

During his reign, Hiel the Bethelite built Jericho. At the cost of Abiram his firstborn, he laid its foundation, and at the cost of Segub his youngest, he set up its gates, according to the word of the Lord He had spoken through Joshua son of Nun.
(1 Kings 16:33-34)

Pay particular attention to that little phrase "at the cost of."

Bad bosses are willing to sacrifice their family and the families of those they lead on the altar of work. Recently, I came across this little poem from an unknown author that captures just how sad this is:

"I have a son who's five years old, a boy, so very fine. When I look at him, it seems to me that all the world is mine, but seldom do I see my son awake and bright. I only see when he sleeps. I'm only home at night. When I come home so weary, the darkness after day, my wife says to me, oh, man, you should have seen him play. So, I stand beside his bed and wonder and ponder if he's dreaming, 'why isn't Daddy here?'"

Bad bosses create environments that sacrifice families on the altar of jobs. We forget that an important leadership goal should be for our team's families to thrive. Bad bosses create environments that force their employees to choose their spouse and kids or career success.

Recently, the youngest of our three children graduated from high school. That means we are now empty nesters! But looking back over the last thirty-plus years of having our children in the house, I have so many wonderful memories. All three of our kids were highly active in sports. We have been to more football, baseball, basketball, and volleyball games than I can count. One of the things I'm the proudest of as a father is that I can count the number of games I missed due to work on one hand. I do not look back on those years and feel the least bit guilty for missing a committee meeting because I was at one of my children's events.

I want to say a word of caution to you as a leader. While you must lead well and grow your organization, you should never do so at the expense of your family. You should also never ask your employees to do it at the expense of their families. God forbid that we build our churches, teams, or businesses "at the cost of" our families.

In his article, *How to Keep Your Profession from Becoming an Obsession*, Rick Warren says, "Work can become an addiction. It's a fix. It's a narcotic. You've got to have it to stay high and you're so afraid if you don't get it, you're going to feel bad. So, you cannot slow down. Like any addiction, you can become so addicted that you ignore your family, you ignore your spiritual development, you even ignore your health."[1]

Don't ignore your family. Don't encourage, or even allow, those you lead to neglect their families, either. Over the years, there have been some practical ways that I've tried to practice this. I've made marriage counseling free to staff members and days off mandatory. When you understand organizational success is a marathon and not a sprint, you will no longer feel the pressure to sacrifice families on the altar of work.

Last but not least, here is the final hurdle to clear if you want to be the worst boss ever:

#3 - Make It All About Yourself

This trifecta will get you into the Bad Boss Hall of Fame: cutting corners in your personal life, encouraging your team to sacrifice their families on the altar of career, and making it all about yourself!

Selfish leadership is a major red flag for all successful bosses. The same qualities which help you lead well can also be used for selfish personal gain. John Acton said, "Great men are almost always bad men."[2] That's because it's always possible to use power and position for our own selfish desire due to our sinful nature. The more powerful a person is, the more evil they can do. Power and control can damage the people who serve an unhealthy leader. The Bible reminds us of this:

> *When the wicked come to power, people hide, but when they are destroyed, the righteous flourish. (Proverbs 28:28)*

That's actually a really helpful good boss takeaway that we should all apply to our lives.

GOOD BOSS TAKEAWAY:

BAD BOSSES ABUSE THEIR POWER, BUT GOOD BOSSES USE THEIR POWER FOR THE GOOD OF THOSE THEY LEAD.

Unfortunately, Ahab failed this test miserably. To highlight that, let me remind you of the classic story of Naboth's vineyard. Ahab had almost everything you could dream of, except one thing that he really wanted. Naboth had nearly nothing besides the one thing Ahab wanted. Based on how the story plays out, Ahab shows us a perfect example of a boss who only cares about himself.

Some time passed after these events. Naboth the Jezreelite had a vineyard; it was in Jezreel next to the palace of Ahab king of Samaria. So Ahab spoke to Naboth, saying, "Give me your vineyard so I can have it for a vegetable garden, since it is right next to my palace. I will give you a better vineyard in its place, or if you prefer, I will give you its value in silver."

But Naboth said to Ahab, "I will never give my fathers' inheritance to you."

So Ahab went to his palace resentful and angry because of what Naboth the Jezreelite had told him. He had said, "I will not give you my fathers' inheritance." He lay down on his bed, turned his face away, and didn't eat any food.

Then his wife Jezebel came to him and said to him, "Why are you so upset that you refuse to eat?" (1 Kings 21:1-5)

Ahab began to covet Naboth's vineyard. It was conveniently located next to Ahab's property and he thought it would be nice to have a vegetable garden right next to his palace. Notice, Ahab had no concern about Naboth's inconvenience. Bad bosses seldom care about how their choices will affect those they lead. They're only ever interested in their own desires.

Ahab started by making an offer that was more than fair. He proposed a land swap, or if Naboth preferred, to purchase the garden with silver. But the Bible says Naboth didn't want to part with the land, which was his father's inheritance. There's no way to know every reason Naboth said no, but there are a few obvious ones.

First of all, Naboth wanted to keep it for personal reasons. It meant a lot to his family, as they had passed it down from generation to generation. To Ahab, the vineyard was just an indulgence. But to Naboth, it was his legacy, identity, livelihood, and his position in the community. It's where his roots were.

Some time ago, my parents had a tough discussion with me about their family farm. They said, "Jackie, we need to have a difficult conversation with you. Neither your sister nor you live close to the family farm. We're getting up there in age, and we're going to have to make a decision about what to do with the farm after we're dead and gone."

That was tough for me to hear because I grew up on that farm. My feet have trod every square inch of it - from the gullies to the hills and valleys. It was not only supposed to be my inheritance, but it was also a part of my identity. It was difficult to think of somebody outside of our family owning the rights to the land.

It was even more difficult for Naboth. He didn't want to sell it for personal reasons, but he also didn't want to sell it for spiritual reasons. Naboth was a devout Israelite. He believed in the word of God. In the book of Leviticus, God specifically instructed the children of Israel not to sell land they inherited from their families. And so, Naboth desired to obey God's instruction. He was more concerned about pleasing God than he was the power-hungry king. In the end, he turned down Ahab's offer, which did not make Ahab happy. Ahab actually had a pity party when he got the news, lying on his bed and refusing to eat.

When I read the story, Ahab reminds me of one of our children when they were young. Without a doubt, whenever their friends would come over to play, their guests would always want to play with our child's toys. And it seemed as if they always picked a toy that our kid rarely played with. Even though they hadn't touched it in a year, it became their favorite all of a sudden. And we never had luck trying to get them to share! They'd run to their room, slam the door, crawl up in their bed, and begin to pout.

That's a picture of what Ahab did when Naboth told him no. He acted like a five-year-old kid who didn't get what he wanted. Somebody should have told him what we told our kids when they were growing up: "You get what you get, and you don't throw a fit." But instead, Ahab threw a massive fit. He was sullen and sad because mean old Naboth wouldn't share his itty-bitty vineyard with him. There he was, the king of the land, pouting like a spoiled child deprived of his favorite toy. He was like a blubbering baby who didn't get his way.

How do you act when you don't get your way as a leader? When things don't go your way, how do you respond?

How we respond when we don't get what we want says a lot about our character. Henry David Thoreau said, "A man is rich in proportion to the number of things he can do without."[3]

At the end of Ahab and Naboth's story, Jezebel swooped in and solved the problem. She ordered Naboth to be killed, and Ahab got his vineyard. He received his new toy at the cost of a man's life who he was called to lead.

What sacrifices are you requiring of others for your personal gain? Do people feel like they are working for you or with you?

GOOD BOSS TAKEAWAY:

GOOD BOSSES BUILD THEIR TEAMS, NOT THEMSELVES.

Simon Sinek says, "Under poor leaders we feel like we work for the company. With good leaders we feel like we work for each other."[4] That is so true! A great leader builds up a team, while a poor leader builds up themselves. A great leader is concerned about others, but a lousy leader is only concerned about themselves.

As you lean into ways to become a better boss, make sure you check your motives at the forefront. Be sure to make others the focus of what you do. When you do, you're able to lead from a place of moral authority that makes your leadership believable and followable. As Albert Schweitzer said, "Example is not the main thing in influencing others, it is the only thing."[5]

So set a good example. Start with your personal life and allow it to leak into your public leadership. You'll be healthier because of it. Those you lead will be healthier because of it. And furthermore, entire families will be healthier because of it!

GOOD BOSS REFLECTION + APPLICATION

Are you the same person in public and private? Ask God to heal the areas of your life that you would be ashamed to share with others.

Do you have a healthy family-work balance? What strategies might help you to leave work at the office and be more present to your family?

How do you respond when things don't go your way? Are you emotionally mature enough to stay composed when you don't get the results you wanted?

AHAB:
THE TELL ME WHAT I WANT
TO HEAR BOSS

"AS GOOD AS IT FEELS, IT IS COMMON KNOWLEDGE THAT FLATTERY IS NOT ALWAYS GENUINE."

Wendy Patrick, Business Insider

Not only is Ahab a case study of a power-hungry boss, but he also created a culture of yes-men. His thirst for power would not allow dissenting voices or competing ideas at the table. He ultimately became the *tell me what I want to hear boss.*

Have you ever had a boss, leader, or pastor like that? One who wasn't comfortable enough in their own skin to allow opposing voices in the room.

Mark this down: bad bosses create environments where healthy descent is discouraged, and uniformity of thought and ideas are expected. In the book, *Why Great Leaders Don't Take Yes for an Answer*, it says, "There is a toll on organizations when leaders fail to create an atmosphere that invites dissent."[1]

Blind uniformity puts a lid on the creativity that healthy descent can provide. If your team thinks the answer is already decided upon before the meeting, they're more likely to shut down and not speak up. This lack of healthy debate and discussion will shutter any great ideas that probably would have come from the team.

Over time, resentment can settle in team members as their opinions aren't valued. They'll begin to grow bitter as they wonder why they were even invited to the meeting in the first place.

This type of culture results in the leader ending up unprotected by the very people who were supposed to protect them. When the leader has a bad idea, it won't be exposed in a room full of yes-people. Instead, that blind spot will go unnoticed and often result in poor decisions and regrettable outcomes that could have been avoided.

Ultimately, the best and brightest on your staff will look for employment elsewhere. Why would they stay when their input isn't requested or listened to? Good leaders won't remain in environments where they aren't actually empowered to lead.

In the end, the leader and organization are placed at risk because truth-telling and reasoned descent were not encouraged. This type of toxic environment is most often created by power-hungry and insecure leaders who desire *blind affirmation* more than *helpful information*.

There isn't a better example than Ahab of a power-hungry leader who demanded blind affirmation over helpful information. That's right - Ahab is so jacked up that he gets two whole chapters dedicated to him in this book!

Recently, they have brought back the game show *The Weakest Link*. My wife and I enjoy it, but I'm always thankful I've never been on the show. If I were, I'm pretty sure I would be the brunt of the host's joke. I'm also positive she would conclude that I am indeed the weakest link. When I read about Ahab compared to all the Old Testament kings, it's clear that he was the weakest link. He was the worst boss ever. And one of the major reasons is that he created a culture of yes-men and women. He developed and led a cesspool of yes-people. He used his power to convince them to never question him and always tell him what he wanted to hear instead of what he needed to hear.

We see a great example of this when Ahab asked Jehoshaphat, the king of Judah, to join him in a war against Aram.

There was a lull of three years without war between Aram and Israel. However, in the third year, Jehoshaphat king of Judah went to visit the king of Israel. The king of Israel had said to his servants, "Don't you know that Ramoth-gilead is ours, but we have failed to take it from the hand of the king of Aram?" So he asked Jehoshaphat, "Will you go with me to fight Ramoth-gilead?" (1 Kings 22:1-4)

We will soon see that Jehoshaphat basically responded by saying yes. But attached to his yes was a caveat. Jehosophat was a much better boss than Ahab, and his leadership was submitted to God. Before they went to war, he wanted to make sure it was the Lord's will.

...Jehoshaphat replied to the king of Israel, "I am as you are, my people as your people, my horses as your horses." But Jehoshaphat said to the king of Israel, "First, please ask what the Lord's will is."
(1 Kings 22:4-5)

Ahab was not concerned about asking his team to communicate the will of God to him. The reason was that he had 400 prophets on his staff that would tell him whatever he wanted to hear. They were a group of yes-men that didn't speak for God. Their only concern was to make the boss happy. Check it out:

So the king of Israel gathered the prophets, about 400 men, and asked them, "Should I go against Ramoth-gilead for war or should I refrain?"

They replied, "March up, and the Lord will hand it over to the king." (1 Kings 22:6)

The prophets didn't consult with God; they were just parroting what Ahab wanted to hear. However, there was one prophet in the nation that still spoke the truth on behalf of God. His name was Micaiah. His voice was a never-ending pain in Ahab's side. He was viewed as a problematic prophet because he told things as they actually were. He wasn't a yes-man; instead, he was God's man. If Ahab truly wanted to serve God, Micaiah would have been a valuable resource to him. Jehosophat wanted to hear what Micaiah had to say, and unsurprisingly, Ahab tried to prevent it from happening.

The king of Israel said to Jehoshaphat, "There is still one man who can ask Yahweh, but I hate him because he never prophesies good about me, but only disaster. He is Micaiah son of Imlah." (1 Kings 22:8)

Did you read that? Ahab said that Micaiah "never prophesies good about me." In other words, he never told Ahab what he wanted to hear. And the same held true in this case. In the end, Micaiah told the king not to go to war as it would surely end in defeat.

The messenger who went to call Micaiah instructed him, "Look, the words of the prophets are unanimously favorable for the king. So, let your words be like theirs, and speak favorably."

But Micaiah said, "As the Lord lives, I will say whatever the Lord says to me."

So he went to the king, and the king asked him, "Micaiah, should we go to Ramoth-gilead for war, or should we refrain?" (1 Kings 22:13-15)

I love Micaiah in this story! He refused to go along with the group of other yes-men, even when they tried to sway him. He vowed to fulfill his duty as a prophet and only relay the message that came from the Lord. And what did the Lord say?

So Micaiah said:

"I saw all Israel scattered on the hills like sheep without a shepherd."

And the Lord said, "They have no master; let everyone return home in peace."

So the king of Israel said to Jehoshaphat, "Didn't I tell you he never prophesies good about me, but only disaster?" (1 Kings 22:17-18)

In the end, Ahab refused to listen to God's voice, listening to the advice he wanted to hear instead. Micaiah's prophecy came true, and Ahab died in battle. It all happened because Ahab created a culture of yes-men and refused to listen to his staff's dissenting voices.

You must understand that a yes-person culture is a massive problem on any team, in any office, or on any staff. Certain dangers come when leaders create a culture of blind yes-men and yes-women, who simply want to go along with whatever the leader wants to do. Let's talk about some of the difficulties of a yes-culture.

YES-CULTURE UNDERMINES HEALTHY CONFLICT

This type of culture undermines healthy conflict. In the story of Ahab and Jehosophat, we find that the confrontation between the prophets was far from healthy.

> *Then Zedekiah son of Chenaanah came up, hit Micaiah in the face, and demanded, "Did the Spirit of the Lord leave me to speak to you?"*
>
> *Micaiah replied, "You will soon see when you go to hide yourself in an inner chamber on that day."*
> *(1 Kings 22:24-25)*

Ahab's prophets wanted Micaiah to play the game and toe the party line. When he didn't, their team got really ugly. As a matter of fact, Micaiah got punched in the face.

Many teams have unspoken expectations that everyone must share the same concepts, ideas, and thoughts. This proves to be problematic because no two people are the same or think the same. So whenever dissenting views pop up, it will negatively affect the harmony and unity of the team. In an unhealthy culture, differing opinions will result in division. And division is never good. Amazingly, the expectation of uniformity will result in a lack of genuine unity.

Unity is one of the most important attributes of successful teams! When I say that you do not need to be a yes-person, I'm not saying that you shouldn't be united with your teammates. Unity is worthy of fighting for even with our differences in personalities, convictions, and leadership styles. The Apostle Paul had some powerful words about unity:

If then there is any encouragement in Christ, if any consolation of love, if any fellowship with the Spirit, if any affection and mercy, fulfill my joy by thinking the same way, having the same love, sharing the same feelings, focusing on one goal. Do nothing out of rivalry or conceit, but in humility consider others as more important than yourselves. Everyone should look out not only for his own interests, but also for the interests of others. (Philippians 2:1-4)

Paul is saying that we should to do everything in our power to value unity. Unity happens when we choose to stick together and move toward God's plan with the help of the Holy Spirit. Unity does not mean a lack of diversity on your team. It's also not uniformity.

It is a beautiful thing to watch a sports team that is working together in unity. They don't all have the same role on the team, but they are working together for the same goal. Take a football team, for example. The job of the center is far different and less glamorous than that of a wide receiver. They have vastly different skill sets, yet they depend on each other to be effective. They aren't a picture of uniformity as they aren't exactly the same. However, they are an amazing picture of unity. It's what Paul was talking about when he said, "fulfill my joy by thinking the same way, having the same love, sharing the same feelings, focusing on one goal."

It's a great thing when a team is intent on one purpose! But it's a terrible thing when there are no dissenting views or opinions about accomplishing that purpose. A successful team values diversity, not division. And that is achieved when the leader values healthy conflict.

I often speak about our team culture and how we value conflict. This leads many people to look at me like I'm strange. I guess I get it - maybe I should start saying we value *healthy conflict* instead. When we gather for meetings, we seldom agree on everything initially. As a matter of fact, almost every time our team gets in a room, we have different opinions, voices, and perspectives. But together, that helps us make better decisions. Healthy conflict makes your team better, not worse.

So what does healthy conflict look like on a team? I think it looks like the following passage:

If your brother sins against you, go and rebuke him in private. If he listens to you, you have won your brother. But if he won't listen, take one or two more with you, so that by the testimony of two or three witnesses every fact may be established. If he pays no attention to them, tell the church. But if he doesn't pay attention even to the church, let him be like an unbeliever and a tax collector to you. (Matthew 18:15-17)

The Bible gives us a very clear prescription for healthy conflict in Matthew. There is a straightforward process that we must go through to maintain unity in the midst of diversity. At the end of almost every staff meeting, we ask if there are any Matthew 18 issues we need to deal with. They might be in our immediate circle or in our broader ministry. God gave us a playbook on how to handle conflict. When you follow it, the relationships on your team grow to be healthier and more supportive.

Perhaps these simple axioms of healthy conflict will help you lift your team in this area:

Axiom #1 - Be willing to punch each other in the face, but never stab each other in the back.

This seems like a pretty polarizing saying, but here's what it means: address your problems with each other face to face instead of behind backs. Create a team culture that's safe to address issues with each other so that you won't gossip about one another. That is what Jesus is prescribing in Matthew 18.

Axiom #2 – We may disagree in private, but we will support each other in public.

Closed-door meetings should be a safe place to question or disagree with the team or leader's direction. This is the place for a healthy dialogue and competing opinions. But keep in mind that at some point, a decision has to be made. Once that happens, public support needs to be apparent, evident, and authentic.

Axiom #3 – Don't bring sheep into shepherd conversations.

This isn't because you want to hide things from the flock or the customer. However, some things would not benefit them to hear. Spiritually immature people should be protected from the frank and candid discussions that must go on behind the scenes to reach the right decisions on difficult topics.

Axiom #4 – The opposite of being a yes-person is not being a no-person.

It's okay to disagree with the team or the leader. But if someone is always colliding with others, they may be the real problem. Although we shouldn't be yes-people, we also shouldn't be Debbie-downers. It can be tempting to take the whole aspirin bottle and over-compensate by disagreeing just to disagree. If you're under the leadership of someone else, it is not your job to make sure that leader doesn't become conceited or prideful. It's your job to figure out what is best for the team and how you can best contribute.

On our team, we have tried to create a culture of positivity, not negativity. We've tried to build a healthy environment even amongst the church's members and attenders. Without being yes-men or women, we want to look for ways to create a yes we can culture.

When I first came to Cross Church, I recognized that we would have to make a lot of changes. Almost every single area of ministry needed a complete overhaul. The way we would come to do things would look nothing like the way members had grown accustom to. Over time, we would change almost everything - our bylaws, building, name, and meeting times. We even transitioned from a single location to a multi-campus model.

If you've ever been a leader before, you know that change inevitably initiates conflict. Before every move, I realized there would be possible conflict; not just in our church, but also on the initial staff I inherited. So right away, I knew we would need to create a yes we can culture. In one of our first staff meetings, I introduced the team to the *YES CAN*. I brought a can into our staff meeting with a big old "yes" written on the outside of it. Every time a team-member deflected, became negative, or was a Debbie-downer, they had to put a dollar in the can. Surprisingly, I earned quite a bit of Starbucks coffee money in those first several years! One staff member even began to put slips of paper that said "I owe you" in the *YES CAN*. But for the most part, our staff did a fantastic job adopting a *yes we can* attitude. It built the foundation which enabled us to reach new heights as an organization.

Years later, I still have that can in my office, but seldom do I earn coffee cash from it. That's because we have a great group of leaders who are looking for ways to say yes to the next big thing God has for us.

We ask our team to look for ways to get to yes without giving over their ability to offer opposing opinions. There is actually a little three-step process that will help you and your team get to yes without being a yes-man or woman:

#1 - Be willing to challenge your initial reaction.

Many times, our initial reaction to a new idea can be negative rather than positive. People can bring up ideas to us as leaders, and our minds go straight to all the reasons it won't work instead of the reasons it might.

As I write this, I'm currently sitting in a Starbucks in Colorado Springs, Colorado, on a Friday morning. It's a pretty big day as the whole family is getting ready for my youngest daughter's wedding. There is a certain finality about parenting that is rushing over me. I have lots of great memories and a few regrets as well. I think the biggest parenting regret I have is centered around saying "no" too often. When our children were young, I was the disciplinarian in our home. As a result, my initial response to any request was almost always no. If I could have a do-over as a father and change anything about my parenting, I would go back and look for more ways to say yes, first. Unfortunately, there are no do-overs, but I guess that's why you get to be a grandparent!

As a leader, I don't want to be like the father who

automatically says no. Therefore, I must be willing to challenge my initial reaction anytime a team member brings a bright new idea to the table.

#2 - Ask them to tell you more about it.

After avoiding your initial reaction, ask your team to tell you more about their idea. Request that they explain more fully, give more detail, and paint a broader picture. This will help you understand their motive and where they're coming from.

#3 - Try to find another version of yes.

Not every idea that people bring to you as a leader should be acted on. However, there might still be a way to achieve the spirit of your team's ideas. That's what I mean by "another version of yes."

For example, let's say you have a staff member that has just read the marketing book, *The Purple Cow*[2]. If you've never read it, the big idea is that marketing should be remarkable and memorable. It revolves around the imagery of seeing a purple cow. You might not remember a brown cow if you drove past one, but you certainly would remember a purple one! You'd probably even park your car on the side of the road and take pictures. Why? Purple cows are remarkable and memorable.

Let's pretend that in response to reading the book, your young, ambitious staff member wants to paint a cow purple and put it on top of the church building. It's an interesting idea but obviously not a feasible idea. But what if there was another version of yes to their idea? What if, instead of a cow on the roof, you could build a new sign that screams, "look at me?" In the end, the spirit of the idea is intact even though you didn't act on the original, slightly crazy, idea.

In review, the first problem with creating a yes-man or yes-woman culture is that it undermines healthy conflict. However, you should not create a no-person culture to avoid a yes-person culture. You should actually do the opposite entirely. You lift the lid off your team's creativity when you develop a *yes we can culture.*

There's the second problem with a yes-culture.

YES-CULTURE AVOIDS HONEST ASSESSMENT

Inherent to a culture of yes-men is the avoidance of honest assessment. I often say that facts are our friends, and feelings our enemies. If the leader thinks everything is going well but doesn't assess factually, there will eventually be problems. Healthy leadership gets down into the mess and mud of their organization. Problems won't go away if you ignore them; they will only get worse.

GOOD BOSS TAKEAWAY:

GOOD BOSSES VALUE FACTS OVER FEELING.

One of the most important things a leader does is define reality. But when that reality is always seen through rose-colored glasses, the entire organization is at risk. Leaders don't need people to tell them what they want to hear, but rather what actually is. It is incumbent for leaders to know what the reality is to make a game plan of where to go from there.

This requires honest, sometimes painful, assessment. But when a leader has honest assessment, they can count the cost before making big decisions. If Ahab had done a better job counting the cost, perhaps his life would have been spared, and the battle would have been won.

Jesus taught us about counting the cost in one of his teachings:

> *"For which of you, wanting to build a tower, doesn't first sit down and calculate the cost to see if he has enough to complete it? Otherwise, after he has laid the foundation and cannot finish it, all the onlookers will begin to make fun of him, saying, 'This man started to build and wasn't able to finish.'"(Luke 14:28-30)*

A good team helps their leader count the cost. *What is the cost of taking action? What is the cost of staying put? When is the right time to move forward?* These are all questions that a leader who values honest dialogue will ask.

A yes-culture will undermine healthy conflict and cause you to avoid honest assessment. Thirdly, it will mess up creative collaboration.

YES-CULTURE SUPPRESSES CREATIVE COLLABORATION

Good bosses develop cultures of creative collaboration. But creativity cannot thrive if everyone is expected to nod their head and tow the party line.

Ed Young's book, *The Creative Leader*, says, "It is no longer merely desirable to develop an organizational culture that embraces new ideas and establishes the structures necessary to implement innovation, it is imperative for the survival of the company."[3]

This is true not only of companies but also of churches. But a yes-person culture is diametrically opposed to a culture of innovation and collaboration. You need to understand as the leader, the best ideas have not yet been heard. Furthermore, they usually aren't yours!

Even the brightest and best leaders need others around them to spur creativity. Think about it - even the great Michael Jordan needed Scottie Pippen and other great team members around him to win six NBA Championships. Jordan's teammates brought skills to the table that he didn't possess. And if the greatest of all time needed others to succeed, then you do too.

Suppose your team comes to a staff meeting thinking a decision has been made before the idea is even pitched. Spontaneity, creativity, and collaboration will never exist. The end result is that your organization will be stunted, at best, and destroyed, at worst. A lack of creative collaboration destroys the entire purpose of a team.

Have you ever heard of a closed-system? It's a physical system that doesn't allow the transfer of matter in or out. I am told that a closed-system will eventually regulate itself to the point of death. If your team has no outside voices or input, then it will eventually regulate itself to the point of death. That's why creative collaboration is so crucial for every team.

I love this little poem. It really makes you think about the value of putting yourself out there, involving others, and making the most of your opportunities:

> There once lived a man who never risked,
> he never tried,
> he never laughed,
> he never cried.
> Then one day when he passed away,
> his insurance was denied.
> They said, since he never really lived,
> then he never really died. – Anonymous

Many of those words are true of teams who have a leader that doesn't cultivate creative collaboration. They don't risk or think outside the box because the leader doesn't expect it or even allow it. Secure leaders encourage competing ideas for the good of the team and for the good of the organization.

In his book, *Doing Church as a Team*, Wayne Cordeiro says, "Secure people encourage others and enjoy their successes. They can appreciate and applaud the achievements of those they have put into positions to succeed. Secure leaders are neither territorial or possessive, they are willing and able to surround themselves with people more qualified than themselves."[4]

I love the idea that a good, secure leader doesn't see creative collaboration as a threat to their leadership. Instead, they see it as a competitive advantage as their team can bring more thought equity to the table than others.

There's one final problem with a yes-culture.

YES-CULTURE ENDANGERS THE LEADER AND THE ORGANIZATION

Ahab's story ends with his brutal death in the battle God told him not to engage in.

So the king died and was brought to Samaria. They buried the king in Samaria. Then someone washed the chariot at the pool of Samaria. The dogs licked up his blood, and the prostitutes bathed in it, according to the word of the Lord that He had spoken. (1 Kings 22:37-38)

Ahab died a death that he would have avoided had he listened to Micaiah. Instead, he created an environment where healthy conflict, honest assessment, and creative collaboration were discouraged. He died, and the dogs licked up his blood all because he surrounded himself with a group of yes-men that couldn't be honest with him, even for his own protection.

THERE WILL BE BLOOD!

There will be blood if you refuse the input and insight

of others. As a leader, suppose you insist on surrounding yourself with people who will tell you only what you want to hear. One day, the dogs will come and lick the blood of you and your organization. Whether quickly or slowly, you will die. Your organization will never reach its potential because its growth was stunted by your unwillingness to broaden your horizons.

If you don't surround yourself with people empowered to be honest with you, your leadership will suffer! You owe it to yourself to refuse the temptation of a yes-culture. Instead, surround yourself with people who will lovingly speak the truth. When you do, your organization will not only avoid pre-mature death, it will thrive!

GOOD BOSS REFLECTION + APPLICATION

Do you have people in your life that are willing to speak tough truths to you? If not, have you given anybody permission to do so?

Does your team push back on your decisions? If the answer is no, consider why that is. They may be leaders incapable of moving the organization forward. Or possibly, you've created a culture of fear.

Do you automatically say no to the ideas of others? Try *finding another version of yes* the next time you're tempted to say no right away.

NINE

ELISHA:
THE BEST EMPLOYEE

WHATEVER YOU DO, DO IT ENTHUSIASTICALLY, AS SOMETHING DONE FOR THE LORD AND NOT FOR MEN.

Colossians 3:23

If you serve underneath someone, this first paragraph is specifically for you. I don't want to ruin your day, but this has to be said: sometimes, the problem at your workplace, church, or on your team is not the bosses' fault. In fact, sometimes it's yours. The truth is, everybody has a boss, whether that looks like a board, manager, or customer. And in the spirit of fairness, we must admit we aren't always as on top of things as we should be. There are days, weeks, or even seasons when we aren't very sharp. Sometimes we don't need our bosses to get things in order; we need to get ourselves in order. We need to sharpen our skills.

Let's continue our journey through the history of Israel's leadership and look at the life of a man named Elisha. Elisha was a prophet who delivered God's messages to Israel during the rule of the nation's corrupted kings. He led a school of prophets where he trained students to do the same miracles God did through him. Through this school, we can learn about the ebb and flow of what working with God looks like. Let's dive in:

The sons of the prophets said to Elisha, "Please notice that the place where we live under your supervision is too small for us. Please let us go to the Jordan where we can each get a log and can build ourselves a place to live there."

"Go," he said.

Then one said, "Please come with your servants."

"I'll come," he answered.

So he went with them, and when they came to the Jordan, they cut down trees. As one of them was cutting down a tree, the iron ax head fell into the water, and he cried out, "Oh, my master, it was borrowed!"

Then the man of God asked, "Where did it fall?"

When he showed him the place, the man of God cut a stick, threw it there, and made the iron float. Then he said, "Pick it up." So he reached out and took it. (2 Kings 6:1-8)

You'd probably agree that this is a rather odd and obscure story. Sometimes I wonder why God chose to include such stories in the Bible. Yet, the prophet losing his ax head gives us a great example of what it looks like to lose your cutting edge at work. The story also provides a formula of how to reclaim it.

Have you ever lost your mojo? Have you ever felt like your get-up-and-go has got-up-and-went? Have you ever felt like you were trying to chop down trees with the handle of a headless ax? If that is your current situation, this chapter is for you! We're going to learn how to get our edge back from the Bible. You don't need a coffee or energy drink; God's way is much more substantial.

REKINDLE THE PASSION FOR WORK

From time to time, we all need to rekindle our passion for the work we were hired to perform. Even if what you're doing is your deepest passion, waning motivation is an inevitable part of human nature. Everyone has seasons when they are just phoning it in and going through the motions.

In our story, it appears that Elisha has started a seminary for upcoming prophets. Because of the success of the school, they ran out of space. As a matter of fact, the enrollment increased so drastically that they needed to build a new dorm. Elisha's school was active, growing, and on the move.

Now let me be very clear, growth is a wonderful thing for any organization. If things are growing and doing well in your business, you're probably pretty happy. If your church is growing, you're probably fired up about what God is doing! But growth always brings certain challenges to any organization. Whenever you start to grow, problems always pop up! And in this case, the problem associated with the school's growth was that the students needed more space.

In our city, the school system can barely keep up with the growth of new students. They frequently need new schools, teachers, and more classroom space. But the tension they face is that they have a minimal budget. I'm sure our local school administrators could tell you about the pains associated with growth.

Over the years, our church has grown. However, there has been lots of hard work behind the scenes to keep up with that growth. We've had to build buildings, increase our staff, pay off debt, enlarge our structures, and fine-tune our systems. That's what I call growing pains! I want you to get this: organizational, personal, and spiritual growth all take a lot of effort and energy.

In work and life, there is no standing still. You are either moving forward or moving backward. If you attempt to put things in neutral, it won't be long before you lose profit or market share at work. It also won't be long before you lose your edge in life. There is no standing still. It's true in every area.

But remember that forward movement can cause friction. If you have children, you're familiar with growing pains. Leg cramps give way to growth spurts, which force you into buying new clothes. And as your children grow, so do expenses! Food, cars, and college all offer challenges for a growing family. The same holds true for businesses, churches, and organizations. The larger you grow, the larger the growing pains become. Enlarging your space, increasing your budget, and expanding your footprint are just a few challenges you may face.

Such was the case with Elisha's school of the prophets. It was growing, and they needed a new dorm. The hand of God was on this school. But when things prosper, one of two spirits will prevail - a spirit of satisfaction or a spirit of sacrifice.

Suppose you lead or volunteer in a church. It can

be a real challenge to sacrifice - building new rooms, opening more services, and increasing your footprint in the community to reach more people for Jesus. If you lead or work for a business, you face the same challenges, just in a different context. But whether you work in ministry or at a secular job, if you are a follower of Christ, you ultimately work for God. Whether you work at a seminary or a steakhouse, you are there to serve God with excellence and joy. The Bible says this:

> Serve the Lord with gladness;
> come before Him with joyful songs. *(Psalms 100:2)*

We are to serve the Lord with gladness. The apostle Paul thought this principle so important that he mentioned it twice in the epistles he wrote:

> Serve with a good attitude, as to the Lord and not to men... *(Ephesians 6:7)*

> Whatever you do, do it enthusiastically, as something done for the Lord and not for men. *(Colossians 3:23)*

That means that regardless of where we work, we are to serve God with a full heart. Our efforts are a service to God, not just our leadership, customers, or congregations. Jesus himself is our boss, and he just happens to be the best boss ever.

Rekindling our passion for our calling starts with remembering that work is a good thing. In fact, it's not just a good thing; it's a God thing! Before God gave Adam a wife, he gave him a job. Before sin entered the world and corrupted everything, work existed in Eden - God's version of paradise. Your work is not evil; it is good. It is a blessing from the Lord. What would happen if you went to work tomorrow with that type of attitude? Every day is an opportunity to work for God and be his ambassador in your workplace!

REMEMBER THE PURPOSE OF WORK

One sure-fire way to rekindle our passion is by remembering the purpose of our work. Work is more about making a difference than earning a paycheck. Let's dive back into our story:

> *"Please let us go to the Jordan where we can each get a log and can build ourselves a place to live there."*

> *"Go," he said.*

> *Then one said, "Please come with your servants."*

> *"I'll come," he answered. (2 Kings 6:2-3)*

The fact that Elisha's students wanted God's prophet to go with them is an indication that they wanted God's presence to go with them. They knew that they would need God to do their work, although it wasn't overly spiritual. And the same is true of you. You need God's presence and instruction in your daily work. Whenever you think you can accomplish without God's help, you're headed for trouble.

To have a purpose in your work, you must make sure you're working within the Lord's plan. That's very, very important, isn't it? God doesn't just want us to work randomly; he has an intentional plan for us. We ought to know that God has a specific purpose for our lives because that's fantastic news. God has specifically planned out your work, even if your job feels mundane. It doesn't matter if you build ships or sermons - God is working through what you do.

I like the attitude of these workers in our story:

"Please let us go to the Jordan where we can each get a log and can build ourselves a place to live there." (2 Kings 6:2)

They wanted to make sure that God was in the middle of their building plans. That's why they asked Elisha, God's prophet, for permission. Too often, we lurch out on our own without asking for God's approval. And then wonder why we are so miserable. Instead of asking God what we should do, we often ask him to bless what we want to do.

Early in the Old Testament, God's prophet represented God himself. And so, the fact that they were speaking to Elisha carried a lot of weight. They were trying to get God's approval through God's prophet. They wanted God involved in the process of what they were building. They understood that God not only wants his work to be done in his might but also in his method.

In other words, we're not only to do what God wants, but we're also to do it the way God wants it to be done. So, before you start building, you need to make sure you have God's building plan. Secondly, and maybe more importantly, is they wanted to make sure they had the Lord's presence. Look at verse three:

> *Then one said, "Please come with your servants."*
> *(2 Kings 6:3)*

They wanted his plan, but they also wanted his presence. They wanted God to be involved with what they were doing. We have not been put on this planet simply to be God's employees. God invites us to work *with* him, not just *for* him. That's a big difference, isn't it? As we work with God, he then works with us. His presence works in us and also through us. That's the way God's work is accomplished. I firmly believe if Elisha had said, "Dudes, I'm not going," the prophets wouldn't have gone either. They would have stayed behind because they wanted to be wherever God was. They wanted to work for God so badly that they were unwilling to work without him.

Our lives would change if we developed an attitude that said, "I'm willing to work for God, but I'm not willing to work without him." Regardless of how gifted you might be, none of us can be effective on our own. We need his presence!

The school of prophets sought God's plan and presence but also accomplished the work together. Purposeful work includes God's plan, presence, and also his people.

So he went with them, and when they came to the Jordan, they cut down trees. (2 Kings 6:4)

Notice the plural pronoun "them." They (plural) came to the Jordan, and they (plural) cut down trees. Follow the progression - God's work is done with his presence, according to his plan, and with his people. That's the joy of serving God together through God's body - the church. God has no hands, but our hands; he has no feet, but our feet. Whenever anything is done for God's glory, his people are somewhere at work in the midst of it.

There is such value and benefit for us when we work together as a team. Honestly, I believe that the real purpose of work might not be the product we create as much as the relationships we build. Yes, it's great to grow your business or church. But growing relationships at your business or church is even more important.

Do you look forward to hanging out with the people at your work? Do you enjoy those relationships? The people you work with might actually be the work God has given you to do. Invest in them, spend time with them, and pray for them.

God's plan, God's purpose, and God's people are all necessary to accomplish God's work. Many times, we convince ourselves of unrealistic limitations by fixating on what we can't do. But God's purpose, presence, and people eliminate those limitations. Maybe it's time to go to work and think about all the things you can do with God on your side!

What then are we to say about these things? If God is for us, who is against us? (Romans 8:31)

I am able to do all things through Him who strengthens me. (Philippians 4:13)

You cannot do God's work without him; but with him, you can do great things. Once we have determined that we have God on our side, our responsibility becomes as simple as this good boss takeaway:

GOOD BOSS TAKEAWAY:

WHEN WE DO WHAT WE CAN, GOD WILL DO WHAT WE CAN'T

Write it down: our responsibility is simply to do our part and trust God with his part. And that is exactly what we see the workers in 2 Kings exemplify. They moved from asking for permission to actively working on the project. They are doing all they can but are suddenly faced with a situation that they don't know how to handle. They must choose if they are going to trust God with the task at hand.

They were flailing away - cutting down trees and dripping with sweat. Keep in mind that even though their work was difficult, there was zero negativity amongst them. There was no inference from God, Elisha, or amongst themselves that they were doing anything incorrectly.

None whatsoever. But in the middle of their obedience, one of the students lost the head of his ax. It plummeted into the water, and the best hope of recovering it was to trust in God.

As one of them was cutting down a tree, the iron ax head fell into the water, and he cried out, "Oh, my master, it was borrowed!"

Then the man of God asked, "Where did it fall?"

When he showed him the place, the man of God cut a stick, threw it there, and made the iron float. Then he said, "Pick it up." So he reached out and took it. (2 Kings 6:5-7)

I'll say it again - this is such a bizarre story. Why did it find its way into the canon of scripture? What can we learn? Notice that the student lost his ax head while he was working. He wasn't lazy, sleeping, or dozing off - he was working hard. But regardless, he still lost it. I have a suspicion that one of the reasons it flew off its handle is because he neglected it to some degree.

I don't know how much time you've spent behind the handle of an ax. But when I was a teenager, my dad hired a friend and me to clean out fence rows. It consisted of chopping down the scrub brush and small trees that grew up into the fence over time. My friend Danny hacked away with that ax tirelessly but accomplished nothing. He had terrible aim and missed the shrub at least three or four times. I stepped in and said, "Danny, let me show you how it's done." I hit the shrub one time with the most perfect strike you'd ever see. And of course, a wasp came out of the shrub and stung me right between the eyes. Needless to say, I did not get any sympathy from my friend.

The guys in our story had spent some time behind the handle of an ax. Notice how they never underwent any training. That's because they had experience. And sometimes we can become so familiar with our work that we can begin to neglect it.

So here is the million-dollar question: when you lose the cutting edge in your life, how do you get it back? Perhaps you've worked at your job for years now. And if you were honest with yourself, you would have to admit that you're probably not as sharp as you once were. How do you get that sharpness back? I would say you get it back just like the boys in our story did. Let's follow their three-step process:

#1 - Realize You Have Lost It

When Elisha's student lost his ax head, he didn't live in denial and just continue to swing the handle. Nope - he took ownership and admitted there was a problem.

Stop pretending and ignoring. You must first realize that you are not as sharp as you once were. Maybe you are exhausted and burned out at work because you are trying to chop down trees without an ax head!

#2 - Admit That It Was Borrowed

Elisha's student was extremely concerned about losing

the ax head because he had borrowed it from someone. In other words, the tool he needed to get the job done didn't belong to him. However, that didn't make it any less necessary.

When it comes to the cutting edge in our work, we must realize that we are using gifts loaned to us from God. We do not possess the power of God in our lives; the power of God possesses us. Understand that God gave you your edge, gifts, and the things that make you who you are. James 1:17 tells us, "Every good and perfect gift is from above, coming down from the Father of the heavenly lights, who does not change like shifting shadows." (NIV) Because all gifts are from God, your talent is on loan!

#3 - Return to the Place Where You Lost It

Then the man of God asked, "Where did it fall?" (2 Kings 6:6)

When we lose the cutting-edge, we need to retrace our steps and figure out when and where we lost it. Another way to talk about the cutting-edge in our lives is by using the word momentum. Most of us don't know how we got momentum in the first place and therefore don't know how to find it when it's gone.

Andy Stanley talks about this issue in one of my favorite teachings. He shares a couple simple components of creating and sustaining momentum. They are invaluable for churches, or people, looking to find or regain this powerful force.

The first component of momentum is **new**. Anything

new you introduce in your ministry automatically triggers momentum. Tweaking something old never generates momentum; it is only triggered by introducing something entirely new.

The second component of momentum is **improvement**. When you start something new, it must be a significant improvement over the old. A slight adjustment won't work - the improvement must be noticeably better.

To sustain long-term momentum, we must keep improving. Long-term momentum is sustained through continuous improvement. You may have heard the saying, "If it ain't broke, don't fix it." That does not apply to the law of momentum! When you've got a great thing going, do not leave it alone. Continuously find ways to tweak it and improve it to sustain momentum.[1]

With that in mind, try to figure out where you lost the momentum in your work life. What did you do to get it? When did you stop doing what gave it to you? What do you need to do to retrieve it?

You can get cutting-edge back for your life and at your workplace! Whether your job is sacred or secular, God wants you to once again be razor-sharp! Just as Elisha helped his student find his ax head, God can help you rekindle your passion and refocus your purpose.

GOOD BOSS REFLECTION + APPLICATION

Are you experiencing any growing pains in your organization? Pray and ask God for a strategy on what steps to take to navigate them.

Is God leading your leadership, or are you doing your own thing and hoping he blesses it? Spend time in his presence and commit to following his methods.

Does your life have momentum? If not, where did you lose it, and what can you do to get it back?

TEN

JESUS: THE BEST BOSS EVER

"IF WE CONDUCTED A SURVEY OF THE DEFINITION OF GREATNESS FOR 21ST CENTURY LEADERS, WOULD THE RESULTS CHANGE? IS GREAT BUSINESS LEADERSHIP STILL ABOUT SETTING A STRATEGIC VISION? OR DO WE CARE MORE ABOUT THE WAY IN WHICH OUR BUSINESS LEADERS TREAT THEIR EMPLOYEES AND THE SOCIETY IN WHICH THEY LIVE? WHAT IS YOUR DEFINITION OF A GREAT BUSINESS LEADER?"

Harvard Business Review[1]

I'm a big fan of sports radio. It's pretty much all I listen to whenever I'm in my truck. Inevitably, each sports season, talk show hosts always bring up the GOAT discussion. In case you don't know, GOAT is an acronym that stands for the *greatest of all time*. So for every sport, there's always a never-ending discussion about who is the best to ever do it. For instance, it is routinely believed that Tom Brady is the greatest quarterback of all time with his six Super Bowl rings. But the discussion gets a little more contentious when you debate the greatest basketball player of all time. Most often, analysts and fans view it as a narrow race between Michael Jordan and LeBron James. Personally, I don't think Danny Ainge gets enough consideration (just kidding!). I tend to lean more toward Jordan, while younger fans seem to side with James.

However, when it comes to discussing the greatest boss of all time, I think the answer is a slam dunk. Clearly, Jesus Christ of Nazareth is the GOAT. Nobody's leadership even comes close to comparing to his. In fact, volumes have been written on his unique skills. He is the antithesis of all the bad bosses we have studied throughout this book. Without a doubt, he is the best boss ever.

So as we look at his life, we won't be learning from his mistakes like the other bosses. Instead, we will learn from his successes.

No wonder the Apostle Paul called him "the King of kings and the Lord of lords." (1 Timothy 6:15) Of all the kings in the Bible, he is the greatest of all time. In fact, the word *lord* in the Greek language has a similar translation to boss. It means supreme authority. Of all the authorities who ever lived, Jesus is the most supreme. There is no discussion or debate needed to establish him as the GOAT!

I love the way Jesus began his leadership. He basically went around asking people to follow him. He started out by adding some key players to his team. We now call those key guys disciples. Disciple is a fancy word that simply means follower. These men followed Jesus, apprenticed under his leadership for three years, and Jesus eventually left the future of the church in their hands.

GOOD BOSS TAKEAWAY:

YOU'RE NOT A LEADER IF NO ONE IS FOLLOWING.

Leadership can be defined in many different ways. However, at the very core, leaders are people who have followers. At the center of Jesus' leadership was a group of men who committed their lives to follow him. It wasn't about an upper-level position or a fancy title. Jesus didn't have those things. He simply led out of who he was, and people bought into it!

Think about this: Jesus asked these men to follow him, and they did. They left their careers and families and followed Jesus wherever he went, doing whatever he told them to do. They sat at his feet and took notes deep into the night. They would hang on his every word and action. There must have been something about Jesus that elicited such loyalty and willingness to follow wholeheartedly. In short, he was a *leader worth following*.

As we wrap up this little book on leadership, it begs the question, are you a *leader worth following*? Like it or not, there is a moral test that great leaders must pass. There must be a goodness about our lives that makes our leadership valuable enough to follow. I'm not suggesting you must be perfect in the same way as Jesus, living a sinless life. That's a goal far too lofty and unattainable. But there must be a moral and ethical quality about your life that gives you the street cred others desire to follow. To be leaders worth following, we must mirror as many of Jesus' positive traits as possible.

Let's look at some of the character traits that made Jesus the GOAT.

HE WAS SECURE

We've already encountered the problems insecurity can bring a leader multiple times in this book. Of all the negative character traits of bad bosses, insecurity is probably at the top of the list. Insecure bosses lead out of fear and jealousy, causing the rest of their team to walk on eggshells. If you don't believe me, ask David about when he played the harp for King Saul and had a spear hurled at him. Some of us know what it's like to dodge the spears of our insecure bosses.

However, the exact opposite could be said of Jesus. He was comfortable in his own skin. He knew who he was and what he was sent to do. In the book of John, we find seven "I Am" statements that Jesus declared about himself:

"I am the bread of life." (John 6:35, 41, 48, 51,) As bread sustains physical life, so Christ offers and sustains spiritual life.

"I am the light of the world." (John 8:12,) To a world lost in darkness, Christ offers himself as a guide.

"I am the door of the sheep." (John 10:7, 9,) Jesus protects his followers as shepherds protect their flocks from predators.

"I am the resurrection and the life." (John 11:25) Death is not the final word for those in Christ.

"I am the good shepherd." (John 10:11, 14) Jesus is committed to caring and watching over those who are his.

"I am the way, the truth, and the life." (John 14:6) Jesus is the source of all truth and knowledge about God.

"I am the true vine." (John 15:1, 5) By attaching ourselves to Christ, we enable his life to flow in and through us. Then we cannot help but bear fruit that will honor the Father.

Was Jesus arrogant and prideful in these declarations about his identity? Absolutely not! He was simply declaring who he was and what he came to do. Jesus never suffered from an identity crisis or led out of insecurity. He never woke up in the morning wondering who he was or why he was there.

This clarity of personhood/godhood allowed Jesus to deal with critics while exuding calm confidence. Think about it: Jesus never seemed to be in a state of hurry or emergency. He responded to each challenge he faced with the grace and confidence of knowing who he was. He had the type of boldness that only security can bring.

How would it change you as a leader or boss if you fully embraced who you are and what you are called to do? Let's break down those two key components of security:

#1 - Who You Are

Secure leaders understand that God has made them exactly as they are for a reason. They get that the most original thing they can be is themselves. They aren't trying to mimic anyone else and don't come across as posers or wannabes.

David was a leader who was more secure than most we read about in the Bible. He wrote about his design in the book of Psalms.

For it was You who created my inward parts;
You knit me together in my mother's womb.
I will praise You
because I have been remarkably and wonderfully made.
Your works are wonderful,
and I know this very well.
My bones were not hidden from You
when I was made in secret,
when I was formed in the depths of the earth.
Your eyes saw me when I was formless;
all my days were written in Your book and planned before a single one of them began.
(Psalm 139:13-16)

Those words are also true of you as a leader. You were created just as you are for a reason. There are no mistakes in your DNA strand. God has made you and wired you with a unique design.

In his book *Younique*, Will Mancini writes, "The difference of identity between any two people in the world is found in less than 1 percent of their DNA. Yet embedded in that 1 percent is jaw-dropping potential for different personalities, beautiful relationships, and bountiful dreams. That 1 percent, together with the peculiar combination of finely detailed surroundings that only you have experienced, ushers in the meaning of being uniquely you."[2]

I love his formula for what makes you, you. Your DNA plus your experiences add up to equal the extraordinary person that you are. You are unique and bring a unique set of gifts to the table.

I know the guys who are reading this will understand the joys of owning a favorite t-shirt. You know what I'm talking about - the shirt you wear that is completely worn out. For years, my favorite t-shirt had these words on the front of it: *I Bring Nothing to the Table.* I wore it every chance I got until it was worn away to nothing. My wife finally secretly threw it out in the trash.

If you go through life wearing a metaphorical I *bring nothing to the table* attitude, you will miss the mark and live far below the poverty line of self-worth. The fact of the matter is that you bring something to the table! That is not arrogance or pride. Believing in what you bring to the table is believing what God has already said about you. Jesus believed in himself and invites us to do the same.

As Martin Buber says, "Every person born into this world represents something new, something that never existed before, something original and unique... Every man's foremost task is the actualization of his unique, unprecedented and never-recurring potentialities, and not the repetition of something that another, and be it even the greatest, has already achieved."[3]

Write this down: you are fearfully and wonderfully made. You are unique. And because of that, you can overcome insecurity by understanding who you are and what you're called to do.

#2 - What You Are Called to Do

Jesus was secure in his calling. He knew both who he was and what he was sent to do. Sometimes our problem is that we can get caught up in the complex instead of focusing on the clear. One thing that will help that is to be laser-focused on what you believe God has called you to do, specifically.

Calling can seem like a difficult thing to nail down. But this might help clear things up: your calling goes hand-in-hand with your gifting. Calling starts with determining what you're good at and considering how you can use your gift to change the world. Your calling most often is found at the intersection of your deepest joy and the world's greatest need. Where joy and need meet is where you need to spend the bulk of your time and attention. Doing this will free you up to live and lead securely, knowing that you are doing what you have been called to do. There's a scripture in the book of Ephesians that explains our unique calling beautifully.

For we are His creation, created in Christ Jesus for good works, which God prepared ahead of time so that we should walk in them. (Ephesians 2:10)

The Greek translation for the word *created* used above is *poiema*. It's where the English word, poem, is derived from. A poem is a work of art that is carefully sculpted and crafted. If you're reading this, you have been carefully sculpted and crafted to do God's good works.

Eugene Peterson writes, "In the life of faith each person discovers all the elements of a unique and original adventure. We are prevented from following in one another's footsteps and are called to an incomparable association with Christ. The Bible makes it clear that every time there is a story of faith, it is completely original. God's creative genius is endless. He never, fatigued and unable to maintain the rigors of creativity, resorts to mass-producing copies."[4]

Say it with me: "You are unique!" When you look in the mirror, realize you are an original! You have permission to be comfortable in your own skin because there is nobody else exactly like you. Like Jesus, you can lead out of a deep sense of personal security and avoid the pitfalls that an insecure boss can bring on others and organizations.

HE WAS ATTENTIVE

Great leaders are listeners, and nobody ever listened better than Jesus. Could you imagine sitting down for a counseling session with him? He would listen to your spoken and unspoken words with a focus and concern that no one else on the planet could.

In John 4, Jesus famously encounters and interacts with a woman at a well. In the scorching heat of the day, she had come to draw water to satisfy her physical needs. But Jesus offered her a different kind of water to quench her spiritual needs. In their brief interaction, Jesus listened to her words, saw her wounds, and offered her hope.

Jesus said, "Everyone who drinks from this water will get thirsty again. But whoever drinks from the water that I will give him will never get thirsty again—ever! In fact, the water I will give him will become a well of water springing up within him for eternal life."

"Sir," the woman said to Him, "give me this water so I won't get thirsty and come here to draw water."

"Go call your husband," He told her, "and come back here."

"I don't have a husband," she answered.

"You have correctly said, 'I don't have a husband,'" Jesus said. "For you've had five husbands, and the man you now have is not your husband. What you have said is true." (John 4:13-18)

In their interaction, we see that Jesus heard what she said, but also what she didn't say. He focused attention on a lady who was far from God but whom he saw great potential in. That's the kind of listening skills we need to cultivate as leaders and bosses. Leaders who slow down enough to hear their people's words and see their wounds create great work environments.

GOOD BOSSES HEAR THE WORDS AND SEE THE WOUNDS OF THOSE THEY LEAD.

To do this, we as leaders must slow down long enough to listen. One of the curses of highly successful bosses is they too often move at the speed of sound. We can buzz by people on our way to the proverbial top. However, one of the great character traits of Jesus was that he walked slowly through large crowds. How would it improve your team or staff if you did the same? How would they respond if you, as the leader, slowed down enough to listen and empathize? Remember, as leaders, we need to listen to the spoken words and the unspoken ones. Our heads should be on a swivel, looking for incongruences on our team and addressing them before creating gaps too large to bridge.

To lead like Jesus, you must slow down and listen like Jesus.

HE WAS HUMBLE

The Bible has a lot to say about the humility of Jesus. Two of my favorite passages regarding his humility are in Philippians and the Gospel of Mark.

Make your own attitude that of Christ Jesus,
who, existing in the form of God,
did not consider equality with God
as something to be used for His own advantage.
Instead He emptied Himself
by assuming the form of a slave,
taking on the likeness of men.
And when He had come as a man
in His external form,
He humbled Himself by becoming obedient
to the point of death—
even to death on a cross. (Philippians 2:5-8,)

The same Jesus that made those bold "I Am" statements in the Gospel of John is the same Jesus who humbled himself and became obedient to death on a cross. Why? Because like any truly great boss or leader, he placed others first. In Mark, Jesus reminds us of the importance of putting others first for the leader.

Jesus called them over and said to them, "You know that those who are regarded as rulers of the Gentiles dominate them, and their men of high positions exercise power over them. But it must not be like that among you. On the contrary, whoever wants to become great among you must be your servant, and whoever wants to be first among you must be a slave to all. For even the Son of Man did not come to be served, but to serve, and to give His life—a ransom for many." (Mark 10:42-45)

Jesus basically turns the whole idea of what it means to be a successful leader upside-down. Bad bosses have a history of dominating and exercising power over those they lead. Not with Jesus. He was the original servant leader.

Servant leadership is a leadership philosophy in which the main goal of the leader is to serve. This is different from traditional leadership, where the leader's main focus is the thriving success of their company or organization. A servant leader puts their employees' needs first, develops them to perform at the highest possible level, and shares their power with them. Servant leadership inverts the norm. Instead of the people working to serve the leader, the leader exists to serve the people.

No one did this better than Jesus, as he even gave his life for those he led. If the organization you are called to lead will become a life-giving force for your team and those you serve, you must adopt this kind of leadership philosophy. However, this cannot be achieved unless you, as the leader, also adopt an attitude of humility.

Another great leader in the Bible, the Apostle Paul, said, "Do nothing out of rivalry or conceit, but in humility consider others as more important than yourselves." (Philippians 2:3) Elevating others above ourselves is a foundational principle for the servant leader.

Jesus' leadership was extremely secure, attentive, and humble. And last but not least, let's dive into how purposeful the best boss ever proved to be.

HE WAS PURPOSEFUL

Jesus' life dripped with purpose and meaning. He knew that he was called to die on the cross, and nothing could distract him from that mission. At the very beginning of Jesus' earthly ministry, Satan tempted him to compromise God's calling and join forces with him instead. Jesus' response to those temptations revealed his heart - one that was dead-set on his Father's purpose.

Often, leaders become distracted with competing visions and opportunities. It's tempting to forfeit God's main purpose for us to focus on ancillary issues. However, as has been said many times, *the main thing is to keep the main thing, the main thing.*

Jesus was locked into *the main thing* from the earliest stages of his life. On one occasion, he even had to remind his parents about the guiding purpose of his life.

"Why were you searching for Me?" He asked them. "Didn't you know that I had to be in My Father's house?" But they did not understand what He said to them. (Luke 2:49-50,)

This sense of divine purpose continued to the very end of Jesus' life.

When the days were coming to a close for Him to be taken up, He determined to journey to Jerusalem. (Luke 9:51)

Did you catch that? He determined to go to Jerusalem. And some not so pleasant things awaited him there. He would experience his crucifixion, which turned out to be the apex of God's purpose for Jesus' life - to die on a cross for the sins of all mankind. Even though his purpose was painful, Jesus never became distracted by more comfortable or glamorous things.

Thankfully, you have not been called to die on a cross for all mankind. That was was a mission unique to only Jesus. However, you have been called to live your life on purpose, keep your eye on the ball, and stay true to your organization's mission.

I'm convinced that leaders who are secure, attentive, humble, and purposeful can finish strong. Your legacy doesn't have to be that of a bad boss. You can lead well and end well. But you must take your cues from the greatest leader of all time - Jesus Christ. The writer of Hebrews challenges us with as much:

> *Therefore, since we also have such a large cloud of witnesses surrounding us, let us lay aside every weight and the sin that so easily ensnares us. Let us run with endurance the race that lies before us, keeping our eyes on Jesus, the source and perfecter of our faith, who for the joy that lay before Him endured a cross and despised the shame and has sat down at the right hand of God's throne.*
> *(Hebrews 12:1-2)*

I love that imagery. The point of running the race is to win the prize, requiring us to run with great purpose. In other words - finish strong! But how do we finish strong? By keeping our eyes on Jesus. If you want to be a better boss, you must look to the best boss ever and lead like him.

This not only applies to our lives as leaders but also to our lives as parents, spouses, and people in general.

Since being a newlywed, I've had a corny vision of how I want my family to turn out. I've shared it with my wife and in sermons. I want to sit on the front porch swing, look out over our yard that is protected by a white picket fence, and watch our kids, grandkids, and great-grandkids play. I believe I'll have the assurance of knowing they're all living for Jesus. With a heart full of gratitude, I'll reach over and grab my wife's age-spotted hand and say, "We did good."

At this point in my life, I'm officially an empty nester. My youngest daughter just recently got married, and I'm a grandpa of three. Having reached this season, there are some important things I'm able to share.

First, it didn't take as long as I thought it would to reach this age. Secondly, it's extremely tough to find a house with a porch swing and a white picket fence in Arizona. Thirdly, my wife aged a lot better than I imagined in my vision. And last but not least, if you want to end well, you must plan well.

Ending well in your business, church, or family requires advanced planning. It demands that you avoid the pitfalls that others have made, especially those we've learned about from the bad bosses in this book. If we continuously give our best effort to be more like the "King of kings, and Lord of lords," we will surely end well. We can't go wrong modeling our leadership after who we might even call the "Boss of bosses."

Certainly, for you to lead like Jesus, you need to know him personally. You can't lead like him if you don't have a relationship with him. I'm so thankful that the Bible clearly teaches us how to meet and know him. We start a relationship with him by repenting of our sin and placing our faith in him alone.

Ken Blanchard wrote the bestselling book *One Minute Manager*[5]. In his personal testimony, he shared that after writing that book, he began to study the life and leadership of Jesus. It was that study that led him to realize his need to surrender his life to Jesus. That surrender made such a profound impact that he would later write the book *Lead Like Jesus.*

If you want to lead like Jesus, you must first know Jesus. Romans talks about how to start a relationship with him.

If you confess with your mouth, "Jesus is Lord," and believe in your heart that God raised Him from the dead, you will be saved. One believes with the heart, resulting in righteousness, and one confesses with the mouth, resulting in salvation. (Romans 10:9-10)

To be the best boss possible, you must know Jesus and also pursue and emulate him. He needs to be the focus of your life. You need to position him in his rightful place of Lord. Becoming more like him should become your daily goal. Watch your mad boss skills grow as you grow closer and closer to the best boss ever.

And last but not least, you need to share Jesus. The greatest need of those you lead is to know Jesus. You have been placed in your unique position to guide people, both by your words and deeds, to know him.

A boss that knows, pursues, emulates, and shares Jesus is indeed a *leader worth following!*

GOOD BOSS REFLECTION & APPLICATION

Do you have confidence in who you are? Furthermore, do you have confidence in what God has called you to do? If not, think about what you're good at and how that skill set can be used to meet the needs of people around you.

What area do you need to improve the most to lead more like Jesus - security, attentive listening, humility, or purposefulness? Ask Jesus to empower you in that area.

Do you have an everyday, active relationship with Jesus? If you want to start one, repeat this prayer: "Jesus, I ask you to come into my heart and forgive me from my sin. I believe that you died on the cross so that I could be forgiven. I accept your sacrifice and a relationship with you. I want to live for and lead like you!"

The bottom line is that we can all become better bosses and leaders. We don't have to go down in the Bad Boss Hall of Fame like some of the guys we've studied. You aren't destined to be Michael Scott or, even worse, Ahab. The very fact that you made it all the way to the end of this book tells me you have what it takes. You are most likely already a leader worth following. However, all of us need to continuously improve on who God has called us to be.

The age-old question is this: *Are leaders born or made?* Clearly, the answer is yes.

All leaders are born - duh! But more than that, they are born with a strand of leadership DNA. God has gifted you with the right personality and skill set to lead. Do you remember our discussion about calling? God has personally *called* you to what you are doing. And remember, calling isn't just for people who work in the sacred world. It's for all of us. Whether you lead in a seminary or steakhouse, you are there because God called you there. Rest in that. Take courage in that. Believe in that.

So yes, leaders are born. But all leaders are also made. That means that the strand of leadership DNA must be fostered and developed in your life. You indeed have a gift, but it must be sharpened. It's like leaving a Christmas present unwrapped under the tree. It can only be helpful to your life when you unwrap it and actually use it. Like a muscle that gets stronger, leadership gets strengthened when you put it through intentional training.

So, keep doing what you're doing. Keep reading, growing, and maturing. And if you aren't doing those things, start! Remember this: If you think you're green, you will grow. But if you think you're ripe, you will rot.

As I have been exposed to high caliber leaders, I've been amazed at the value they place on continued development. No matter the field of expertise, great leaders are always looking for the next edge to help them travel further down the road.

What are some ways you can develop your leadership DNA?

#1 - Get Coaching

Coaching has been known to boost confidence, improve work performance, and build effective communication skills. As my personal coach says, "Professionals get coached, amateurs don't." The highest-profile leaders are getting coaching from someone else. If they need it, why should you be any different?

2 - Ask Questions.

The best leaders I know are always asking a lot of questions. My friend and fellow pastor Brian Bowman is the most voracious question-asker I've ever met. He has developed the art of asking the right questions. You will be surprised what you find out when you go through life with an inquisitive spirit.

#3 - Read Books

One of the things I've discovered is that reading books outside of your primary field of expertise is extremely helpful. If you're a pastor like myself, you may be tempted to only read in the religious section of the local bookstore. However, you will be amazed at how much you can learn from books on history, science, business, and marketing. Always be looking for transferable principles that will help you lead.

Again, the bottom line is that we can all become better bosses and leaders. When I think about improving my leadership skills, a whole bunch of *c-words* come to mind. Competency, consistency, coaching, clarity, and courage - the list could go on and on. But let's all agree that for us, Christian leaders, the number one c-word to employ into our leadership is Christlikeness! If we want to be the best boss, how can we possibly go wrong by becoming more like the Best Boss Ever?

NOTES

Introduction

1. Jeff Iorg, *The Painful Side of Leadership: Moving Forward Even When It Hurts* (Nashville, TN: B&H Publishing, 2009).

Chapter 1

1. Perry Noble, *Unleash!: Breaking Free from Normalcy* (Carol Stream, IL: Tyndale House Publishers, 2012).
2. Joe Fehrmann, "The Pike Syndrome," *The Rainmaker Companies.* December 13, 2018. https://therainmakercompanies.com/featured-news/the-pike-syndrome-2/

Chapter 2

1. Jan Winebrenner, Debra Frazier, *When a Leader Falls: What Happens to Everyone Else?* (Ada, MI: Bethany House Publishers, 1993).
2. Gordon MacDonald, *Ordering Your Private World* (Nashville, TN: Thomas Nelson Publishing, 2012).
3. MacDonald, *Ordering.*
4. Rod Handley, *Character That Counts - Who's Counting Yours?: Growing Through Accountability* (Omaha, NE: Cross Training Publishing, 2012).
5. "On this date: The Modesto Manifesto," *The Billy Graham Library.* October 24, 2017. https://billygrahamlibrary.org/on-this-date-the-modesto-manifesto/
6. Lou Holtz, "When people need love and understanding," *BrainyQuote.com.* https://www.brainyquote.com/quotes/lou_holtz_664701

204

Chapter 4

1. John Acton, "Lord Acton Quote Archive," *Acton Institute*. https://www.acton.org/research/lord-acton-quote-archive (December 19, 2020).
2. MacDonald, *Ordering*.
3. Handley, *Character*.
4. MacDonald, *Ordering*.

Chapter 5

1. Alexander McLaren, "Commentary on 1 Kings 12:4," Alexander McLaren's Expositions of Holy Scripture. https://www.studylight.org/commentaries/mac/1-kings-12.html
2. Steve Saccone, *Relational Intelligence: How Leaders Can Expand Their Influence Through a New Way of Being Smart* (San Francisco, CA: Jossey-Bass, 2009).
3. Tim Sanders, *The Likability Factor: How to Boost Your L-Factor and Achieve Your Life's Dreams* (New York, NY: Three Rivers Press, 2006).
4. Tony Dungy [@TonyDungy], "Why would you find it hard to believe that the Holy Spirit could speak to Nick Foles" [tweet], February 6, 2018. https://twitter.com/tonydungy/status/960906784696406016?lang=en

Chapter 6

1. Robert I. Sutton, *Good Boss, Bad Boss: How to Be the Best…and Learn from the Worst* (New York, NY: Hachette Book Group, 2010).
2. Aung San Suu Kyi, Freedom from Fear (New York, NY: Viking Books, 1991).
3. Simon Sinek, *Together Is Better: A Little Book of Inspiration* (New York, NY: Penguin Random House, 2016).

Chapter 7

1. Rick Warren, "Leadership Lifter: How to Keep Your Profession From Becoming an Obsession," *Purpose Driven Small Group Network.* January 28, 2010. https://pdsgn.wordpress.com/2010/01/28/leadership-lifter-how-to-keep-your-profession-from-becoming-an-obsession/
2. Acton, "Lord Acton Quote Archive."
3. Henry David Thoreau, *Walden* (Princeton, NJ: Princeton University Press, 2004).
4. Simon Sinek [@simonsinek], "Under poor leaders we feel like we work for the company" [tweet], April 20, 2015. https://twitter.com/simonsinek/status/590165880752996354?lang=en
5. Albert Schweitzer, "Example is not the main thing in influencing others," BrainyQuote.com. https://www.brainyquote.com/quotes/albert_schweitzer_112973

Chapter 8

1. Michael Roberto, *Why Great Leaders Don't Take Yes for an Answer: Managing for Conflict and Consensus* (Upper Saddle River, NJ: Pearson Education, 2013).
2. Seth Godin, *The Purple Cow: Transform Your Business by Being Remarkable* (New York, New York: Penguin Group, 2003).
3. Ed Young Jr., *The Creative Leader: Unleashing the Power of Your Creative Potential* (Nashville, TN: B&H Publishing, 2006).
4. Wayne Cordeiro, *Doing Church as a Team: The Miracle of Teamwork and How it Transforms Churches* (Bloomington, MN: Bethany House Publishers, 2015).

Chapter 9

1. "Andy Stanley Shares Three Components of Momentum," *Orange Leaders Blog,* August 5, 2014. https://orangeblogs.org/orangeleaders/2014/08/05/momentum/

Chapter 10

1. Tony Mayo, "Defining Greatness," *Harvard Business Review*, July 10, 2007. https://hbr.org/2007/07/defining-greatness-1

2. Will Mancini, *Younique: Designing the Life that God Dreamed for You* (Nashville, TN: B&H Publishing, 2020).

3. Mancini, *Younique*.

4. Mancini, *Younique*.

5. Kenneth Blanchard, Ph.D., Spencer Johnson, M.D., *The One Minute Manager* (New York, NY: William Morrow and Company, 2003).